THE LIVING ART OF
Bonsai

Walter Liew

ISLAND HERITAGE™
PUBLISHING

ISLAND HERITAGE™
P U B L I S H I N G
A DIVISION OF THE MADDEN CORPORATION

94-411 Kō'aki Street, Waipahu, Hawai'i 96797-2806
Orders: (800) 468-2800 • Information: (808) 564-8800 • Fax: (808) 564-8877
islandheritage.com

ISBN 1-59700-185-6
First Edition, First Printing - 2007

Photography by Romeo Collado

Contents

Introduction 04

I. History:
Chapter 1. History of Bonsai 10

II. Design:
Chapter 2. Styles 18
Chapter 3. Composition 72

III. Technique:
Chapter 4. Materials and Tools 88
Chapter 5. Create a Bonsai Step-by-Step 94
Chapter 6. Training and Shaping 96
Chapter 7. Wiring 104

IV. Growth and Maintenance:
Chapter 8. Tree Identification and Care 112
Chapter 9. Parasites, Pests, and Fungi 121

V. Other Elements:
Chapter 10. *Jin* and *Shari* 128
Chapter 11. Rock and Stone 134

Epilogue 142

Appendices:
A. Glossary of Terms 144
B. Judging Bonsai 145
About the author 147
Bibliography 148

Introduction

During the last five decades I have been trained by bonsai masters of China and Japan. Traveling in the United States, Asia, and Europe, seeking out bonsai hobbyists, I have found that few people outside Asia fully understand bonsai or know how to create one of a quality aesthetic. Many believe a bonsai is simply a dwarfed, aging tree or shrub planted in a pot, which requires only regular fertilizing and watering to keep it healthy. This is not bonsai. Bonsai are continually being trained and shaped, aesthetically wired and bent to achieve specific styles and forms, fulfilling strict criteria. They become old. They have the illusion of trees in the wild. This is the concept of bonsai.

In essence, bonsai is a miniature tree or shrub grown in a pot that possesses every element and characteristic of natural beauty of the larger tree in the wild. A good bonsai puts the viewer in touch with nature.

Right: Hybrid Purple Bougainvillea
Nyctaginaceae Spectabilis • Eccentric Style
43 years old • 35" x 38"

Bonsai is a uniquely living art, and is always to be regarded as an unfinished art. Regardless of its age, a bonsai can always be improved on in the hands of a master, whereas other art forms may be more generally regarded as completed.

While I have participated in numerous bonsai expositions over the years, I have found the art of bonsai is often misrepresented. Although an exhibitor may possess superb horticultural skill or present beautiful-looking trees, there are often specific style criteria missing.

The fulfillment of style in bonsai is as important as the fulfillment of required elements in a figure-skating competition — these elements are essential to each art form.

A bonsai is not naturally dwarfed, nor has the tree been treated by any chemical agent to stunt its growth. Trees chosen for bonsai are grown under training conditions until they reach a desired size and shape before being transferred to a bonsai pot. A bonsai must primarily be kept outside and cannot be a permanent indoor plant. (However, to mature a tree quickly, you may plant a bonsai in the ground temporarily, then return it to its pot for permanent display.)

Bonsai require the same conditions when in a pot as in the wild. In fact we use nature to our advantage to keep bonsai small. The sun's ultraviolet rays break down growing nutrients and wind ventilation allows moisture evaporation, thus slowing the tree's growth. The tree is trimmed and buds nipped to promote twigging and new foliage in proportion to the rest of the tree. The root system is also stimulated by trimming. Limiting growth by these measures keeps the tree small but healthy and beautiful. By continuous repetition of these techniques, the tree gradually and aesthetically refines into an idealized form. In the words of John Keats, this can be "a thing of beauty" and "a joy forever."

Left: Surinam Cherry
Eugenia Uniflora
Umbrella Style
20 years old
15" x 18"

Right: Bird Plum
Sageretia Theezans
Slanted Style
57 years old
30" x 30"

History

Banyan • *Ficus Retusa* • Eccentric Style • 78 years old • 46" x 39"

History of Bonsai

The cultivation of plants and herbs in containers was practiced by the ancient Greeks, Romans, Babylonians, Persians, Egyptians, Anglo-Saxons, and others. However, whether this horticultural methodology became the aesthetic art form we know today as bonsai is largely conjecture. Without a historical continuity of details to establish its evolution, bonsai's origins among these cultures must be considered unknown.

In China, on the other hand, there is a long history of container horticulture leading up to the bonsai form. Merging significant historic developments over several thousand years, Chinese container horticulture embodies spiritual and aesthetic values that transcend the pragmatic purposes of potting plants and herbs.

As early as the third millennium BC, Wong-Dee, "the Yellow Emperor," popularized the use of extracts of specific plants as medicinal cures for different human illnesses. Perhaps for the convenience of herbal doctors of the time, potting valued medicinal plants and herbs ensured their supply when out of season and in nonnative or indoor environments. In the earliest Hsia, Shang, and Chou dynastic periods (2205–256 BC), container planting existed on an extensive scale and included herbs, flowering plants, and small fruit trees. Among the ruling and intellectual classes of the Chou dynasty (1150–256 BC), feng shui added impetus to container horticulture within the home. Feng shui masters of the time taught that through an understanding of how to live well, eat well, and move well through exercising the body, one could achieve a longer and more intellectually productive life. The teachings claimed there was special value in surrounding oneself within the home or place of study with flowering plants and potted herbs—not

An immortal collecting ling-ehih (MANNA)
By Yen Hung-Tzu, Ching Dynasty

only as interior decoration but for their added life force and ability to counteract polluted household air with fragrance and photosynthesis. Feng shui masters believed such practices were personally pleasing to one's spirit.

In neighboring India, there was a significant tradition of dwarfing trees with a primarily medical purpose. This science was called *vaamanta nu vrikshaddi vidya* (*vaaman* meaning "dwarfed"; *tanu*, the "body" or "trunk"; *vrikshaddi*, "tree"; and *vid ya*, "science"). Practitioners who relied on the medicinal properties of large trees that grew only in remote forests at a great distance could instead use extracts from dwarfed versions of these trees. A footnote to bonsai history can also be found in the military conquests and extended tributary relationships of ancient China. During the Han dynasty (206 BC–AD 221), one of China's five neighboring tribes became particularly militant and hostile. These were the Hsiung-nu (Huns), whom the Han emperor attacked with

Social meeting of Sung scholars
Ancient Palace Museum Collection

The Boki Ekotoba picture scroll
Aged miniature trees in pots are displayed on single-legged stands, while sand covers the earth of the pots.

a massive cavalry, driving them deep into central Asia and beyond. (Their further migration over a century later would bring them into eastern Europe, where they came to be called Hungarians.)

The victorious Han annexed the vast area of eastern Turkistan once dominated by the vanquished tribe, where they discovered a variety of foreign fruit trees, vegetables, and flowers, and brought them back by the cartloads. A special value was attached to these war prizes and they began to appear in the imperial gardens of central China, thousands of miles from their origins and often in an unfavorable new environment. Container planting was typically adopted to control their habitat and enhance the success of their survival.

Soon, poets and artists ascribed spiritual values to these trophies of war, such as the peony flower becoming the symbol of China.

Not long after, the earliest Buddhist temples and monasteries were decorated with potted trees and plants. The horticultural practices of these forest monasteries attest to the spiritual and intellectual satisfaction the ancients derived from container gardening.

A scholar and honorable politician
Tao-Yuan Ming (365-427) enjoying his potted chrysanthemum.
By Chen, Hung-*Shou*
Ming Dynasty (1368-1644)
Ancient Palace Museum Collection

The earliest known written record of the word *bonsai* is believed to be in the ode "Returning Home," by Eastern Chin of Six Dynasties (222–589) scholar Tao-Yuan Ming (365–427). The poem expresses the politician's aim to resign from a government he has served long and honorably, and to return to the peaceful village life of his boyhood. He proposes to do nothing more than cultivate chrysanthemums and bamboo in pots and live a simple, contemplative life.

About three hundred years later, in the beginning of the Tang dynasty (618–906), Japanese emissaries returning from China would cause a wave of infatuation with China's contemporary lifestyle among Japanese intellectuals. The Buddhist Ch'an (Zen) monk Raukei Doryu besieged Japan with such teachings, and a new wave of Chinese culture and arts was infused into the country.

At this time in China, a libertine break from the rigidity of classical Chinese tradition was occurring, as seen in Chang-Tse Yuan's painting *Peeping at Bath*, which depicts Emperor Tong-Ming Huang (712–756) peeping at his beautiful consort Yang-Kuei Fei taking her bath. Of interest in this realistic glimpse of contemporary domestic life is a bonsai on the bathroom floor, thought to be the earliest painting of bonsai. Numerous later paintings of this era (seen today in the Ancient Palace Museum collections in Taipei and Beijing) show pine, cypress, plum, orchid, chrysanthemum, and bamboo—all planted in containers. Both bonsai and *suiseki* (stone in a pot or on a wooden stand) are mentioned in poems and prose of the times, as the horticultural practice became a pastime of the leisure class.

Listening to the music of a fair lady
By Tan Yin of the Ming Dynasty
Ancient Palace Museum Collection

Sung scholars gathering, by Yeo, Wen Han. Painted in 1752.
Ancient Palace Museum Collection

An illustrated book on potted dwarf trees from the Sung dynasty (960–1279) displays specific bonsai styles, including pagoda, earthworm, dancing dragon, windswept, flattop, and forest planting. In the Kian Lung time (1736–1796) of the Ching dynasty (1644–1911), Chinese scholars and artists of the Young-Zhou school created their own bonsai styles— formal model, slanted model, cascade, raft, literati (a refinement of the literati style that emerged in the twelfth and thirteenth centuries), rock cling, and umbrella—and recorded each with a drawing. These styles are still recognized today.

Famous bonseki
By Chang, Jiea-Den of the Ching Dynasty
This rock is still located at Tin-Zhou of North China. It is worshipped by Sung Shalan Su, Tung-Poa.
Ancient Palace Museum Collection

Although introduced to Japan during the Tang dynasty, bonsai as an art form failed to develop much interest there until the Yuan dynasty (1280–1363), when Japanese merchants, traveling scholars, and students reached China and learned firsthand of its contemporary culture and arts. This led to a greater infusion of bonsai and *suiseki* in Japan, which developed into a widely popular pastime.

Japan's Tokugawa period (1603–1867) was a long era of peace, prosperity, and relative isolation from outside influence, bringing a rise to domestic arts and crafts and a flourishing of landscape gardening.

A centerpiece for New Year's Day
By Chen Shu of the Ching Dynasty
Ancient Palace Museum Collection

A picture from *Utamaro's Koraku Zu* (*Picture of Pastimes*, circa 1800), shows a distinguished-looking pine in a pot with a design of dragons in relief.

Bonsai culture developed further, particularly during the reign of Shogun Tokugawa Iemitsu, who had a great personal love of bonsai. (His favorite was a five needle pine, which, at over three hundred years old, can still be seen today in the Imperial Garden at Kyoto.)

Due to the country's isolationist policy during this period, many scholars clung to a single prevailing style—the free-spirited *bunjin*, or *nauga*, also called the southern Chinese form or Linghan style. This style is said to have derived from the milder subtropics of southern China and its much longer growing season than in the north. This permitted bonsai workers in the Kwang-tung province to introduce a "cut and grow" method, which was inspired by the contemporary Chinese brush painting they practiced.

Look closely at the woodblock prints of Hokusai Katsushika (1760–1849) and Hiroshige Ando (1797–1858), who both worked in this style.

Their trees appear in literati-style landscapes and are slender trunked with a fine taper, graceful even when at sharp, tortured angles.

Japan's Emperor Meiji (1868–1912) was a gifted poet with a personal appreciation for bonsai. Through his influence, bonsai was adopted by the intellectual class and connoisseurs to such an extent, it virtually became the semiofficial art of Japan. Bonsai became a common-vernacular Japanese term. The word *bonsai* is actually a Japanese pronunciation of the characters for "tray," "pot," or "dish," and for "tree" or "plant." The characters are common to both Chinese and Japanese, but are pronounced "pone-sigh" in China and "bone-sigh" in Japan.

Twentieth-century China brought many challenges to the

"The Potted Trees Parodied" (*Miiae Hachi-No-Ki*) A woodblock print by Harunobu Suzuki.

preservation of classic artistic treasures, including bonsai. This was a time of loss of what had been an enduring classic culture and a class of scholars for whom aesthetic expressions of life and nature were a way of life. After the collapse of the last Chinese dynasty in 1911, more than twenty restless years of internal warring were then followed by years of Japanese military occupation. Many national treasures were destroyed or damaged while relocating them for protection, or taken away to Japan. Finally, the anti-intellectualism of China's Cultural Revolution (1966–1976) swept away any remaining vestiges of

Chinese tradition judged to be classist or bourgeois. Aged scholars, teachers, and those with intellectual pursuits were all suspect in modern China and were either murdered or dispersed to farming communities in the countryside. Bonsai trees many centuries old were neglected and perished in

Woodblock print by Hokusai (1760-1849)
The Japanese Nobleman Abe No Nakamaro (698-770) is seated on the terrace of a Chinese palace. Nakamaro had accompanied a Japanese envoy to China, which had been sent to obtain the secrets of the system invented in China for calculating time.

this new spirit of harsh pragmatism. Today there is very little remaining bonsai culture in China.

It was the Japanese who introduced bonsai to the Western world at international exhibitions in Paris (1879) and London (1910). In Japan, the first bonsai show was organized in Tokyo in 1914 and has since become a popular national event. Bonsai appreciation has spread to every class of people in Japan. Twentieth-century Japanese who immigrated to the West and returning American GIs who were exposed to bonsai during the occupation of Japan after World War II have also accounted for a universal appreciation of bonsai associated with the Japanese tradition. Yet only recently has a more comprehensive historical perspective recalled the older Chinese origins of bonsai, steeped in its philosophical and aesthetic traditions.

The art of bonsai was introduced to Europe in the Japanese pavilion at the 1878 world fair in Paris and described in the *journal hebdomadaire.*

Design

Chinese Elm • *Ulmus Parvifolia* • Literati-Formal-Model Style • 35 years old • 29" x 31"

Styles

o be a bonsai, each tree must attain an individual style and meet the criteria of that style. If a tree lacks style criteria, it is not a bonsai.

In this chapter, I emphasize thirteen styles:

- Formal Model
- Semi-Cascade
- Literati
- Twin Trunk
- Rock Cling
- Willow and Weeping
- Forest Planting

- Slanted Model
- Full Cascade
- Umbrella
- Exposed Root
- Raft and Root Link
- Eccentric

Formal Model

Formal-model bonsai is considered the most beautiful model. It became popular among scholars and intellectuals in China during the Kian Lung time. Almost a half century later, the style reached Japan.

"The classic pine," an example of formal model seen in a Japanese bonsai instruction manual published in 1829, was considered the most classical of all bonsai styles. However, its tortured angles and sharp tapers of the trunk are very difficult to achieve, so it never became popular, instead remaining dormant in Japan for more than one hundred years. As noted in *Easy Guide to Bonsai*, published in Japan in 1955, "Moyo-Gi [formal model] cannot be classified with any of the other styles discussed . . . eschewing the vulgarity of Slavish adherence to particular rules for training the tree, it aims at something more sophisticated, training the individual tree freely in accordance with its own characteristics so as to bring out its special flavor to the fullest."

While the trunk is curved and tapered, the apex, or tip, is positioned vertically atop the tree, so its shape forms a symmetrical triangle. The roots radiate out in different directions, as with all bonsai styles.

Most sophisticated and beautiful, this style represents tranquility and stability.

Hybrid Pink Bougainvillea • *Nyctaginaceae Spectabilis* • Formal-Model Style • 43 years old • 35" x 42"

Crape Myrtle • *Lythraceae Lagerstroemia Indica Speciosa* • Formal-Model Style • 39 years old • 29" x 34"

Russian Elm • *Zelkova Serrata Makino* • Formal-Model Style • 42 years old • 33" x 31"

Left: *Bougainvillea Nyctaginaceae Spectabilis*
Formal-Model Style
20 years old
25″ x 26″

Right: Lime Berry
Triphasia Trifolia
Formal-Model Style
12 years old
19″ x 17″

Taiwanese Banyan • *Ficus Retusa* • Formal-Model Style • 15 years old • 18" x 19"

Juniper • *Cupressaceae Juniperus Communis* • Formal-Model Style • 25 years old • 33" x 30"

Slanted Model

This form depicts a tree growing away from the direction of strong winds. If grown in shade, it will lean away from whatever is shading it to reach out for light.

The slanted-model trunk leans extremely toward one side with three or four sharp-angled curves. However, it is the position of the apex on one side of the pot that distinguishes this style as "slanted." The tree is planted off center, so the base of the trunk is, for example, to the left if the tree slants to the right, or vice versa, forming an asymmetrical or obtuse triangle. Another important characteristic of this style is the way the roots anchor the leaning tree. Compressed roots are on the side of the slant to buttress the tree.

Long, smooth roots are on the opposite side of the slant to give the appearance of the tree being pulled.

The slanted model represents instability and uneasiness or motion.

"San Jose" Juniper • *Cupressaceae Juniperus* • Slanted Style
20 years old • 31" x 23"

Banyan • *Ficus Microcarpa* • Slanted Style
17 years old • 19" x 17"

Chinese Elm • *Ulmus Parvifolia* • Slanted Style • 28 years old • 26" x 22"

Semi-Cascade

The semi-cascade depicts a tree that in nature grows on or near a vertical rock face or beside a river or lake, where light reflects off the water to the underside of the branches, encouraging the lower branches to extend over the water.

The semi-cascade may be a formal model with the lower branches tipping down, or a tree head that tips down itself with no branches. If a formal model, the lowest branch should almost reach the bottom of the pot.

The semi-cascade trunk starts to grow upward from the soil, but then turns downward in a line that lies between a forty-five-degree angle and just below horizontal, terminating just below the pot rim but not below the pot base. The semi-cascade style is placed in a deeper pot than other styles.

This style represents peacefulness.

Chinese Elm • *Ulmus Parvifolia* • Semi-Cascade Style
17 years old • 25" x 22"

Juniper • *Cupressaceae Juniperus Communis* • Semi-Cascade Style • 55 years old • 38" x 27"

Full Cascade

This form depicts a tree clinging to a cliff face, where it is shaped by snow, wind, and rock fall. Similar to the semi-cascade's downward direction, the full cascade's trunk dramatically curves and tapers, with an apex inverted directly below the center of the trunk, terminating below the bottom of the pot. It is much like water cascading down a waterfall.

The full cascade represents humility.

Juniper • *Cupressaceae Juniperus Communis* • Full-Cascade Style
43 years old • 29″ x 39″

Chinese Elm • *Ulmus Parvifolia* • Full-Cascade Style • 59 years old • 26" x 37"

Literati

What is the meaning of literati (in Japanese the term is *bunjin*, or *penjing* in Chinese)? You must first understand the tradition of China's social advancement. In ancient times, one way to advance socially was by the family-based feudal system. Sons were entitled to their fathers' position and wealth. In this way, the reigning family stayed in power.

The second way to advance socially was to pass the nationwide examination on the classics, which encouraged copying the old masters and perpetuating styles accepted for thousands of years. For men who wished to gain a government position, they had to first master literature, history, philosophy, and the arts and become adept at intellectual gymnastics. When they passed their exams, they were named "literati"—men of letters.

During the twelfth and thirteenth centuries, some of these scholars became disenchanted and removed themselves from the court to live in retreat in Soochow and Hangchow, where the literati flourished. The literati man lived frugally and ascetically, spending most of his time studying and practicing various arts. In time, he turned to sculpture and shaping trees that grew in the courtyards and monasteries. Part of an elite and learned class, the literati's taste was extreme and not accepted by the general public. The bonsai that resulted similarly appeared like an ascetic

Point Banyan • *Ficus Microcarpa* • Literati Style
28 years old • 26" x 25"

monk—tall and thin and embodying the abstract beauty of calligraphy, while still suggesting the rugged and gorgeous nature of the wild.

The literati style of bonsai specifically developed from literati paintings of the Young-Zhou school of landscape painting in the Kian Lung period. These paintings emphasized the grandeur of nature with people in a subordinate role, such as traveling up a path or fishing by small huts. The style used quick calligraphic brushstrokes to depict objects impressionistically rather than realistically or studiously detailed. Much *kunkan*, or empty space, was left to allow for the viewers' own interpretations of the art.

When translated to bonsai, literati became a style of no style, a rule of no rules. It represents balance and beauty—some of the most difficult elements to achieve.

This literati's form suggests a strong brushstroke, like those of the famous landscape painter Shitou of the late Ming dynasty. His trees featured an important element—*kunkan*, a hollow trunk or empty space where the imagination of the viewer can take over. For example, a hollow trunk and striped apex evoke visions of a once-proud tree struck by lightning; a slender tree with a grotesquely twisted trunk is struggling to survive on a steep crag, and is unbalanced and looks dangerous. However, after a few years of work, it becomes well balanced and a handsome literati.

Chinese Elm • *Ulmus Parvifolia* • Literati Style • 48 years old • 34" x 44"

Taiwanese Banyan • *Ficus Retusa* • Literati Style • 18 years old • 21" x 23"

Umbrella

This style was once considered the most difficult to shape, and for a long time bonsaists had a hard time finding trees in nature suitable for this style. However, as my practice, if a bonsai I have been shaping for many years turns out to be a disappointment or does not meet the style's requirement, I cut off all the lower branches and restyle as an umbrella. Usually within a short time, all

The root structure spreads in all directions and is visible above the surface of the soil, as with other bonsai styles.

A good umbrella design has a trunk like that of a formal model—tapered and curved. The apex is round and canopied like a large rice bowl turned upside down.

the nutrients now concentrated in the top will make the crown grow fuller. You do not see the umbrella in any Japanese bonsai books before 1955. A good specimen is still rare in any part of the world.

The canopy of the umbrella-style bonsai represents the sky and heaven. The roots radiate out into a round pot, which symbolizes Mother Earth. The trunk, with all its curving, twisting, gnarling, and aging, is the human being reaching toward the sky, which holds the mysterious and sacred secrets of the universe. The umbrella-style bonsai represents universal secrets.

Banyan • *Ficus Retusa* • Twisted-Umbrella Style • 40 years old • 27" x 27"

Torch of Thai • *Bougainvillea Spectabilis* • Umbrella Style • 38 years old • 29" x 21"

A trunk that is twisted and tapered like the one in this picture is considered a good model of the umbrella style but is very hard to achieve.

Golden Gate Banyan • *Ficus Nerifolia Regularis* • Above-Root-Umbrella Style • 83 years old • 36" x 32"

Calamondin • *Citrus Mitis* • Umbrella Style • 24 years old • 23" x 22"

Golden Dew Drop • *Duranta Repens* • Umbrella Style • 8 years old • 26" x 22"

Twin Trunk
(God and Son / Father and Son / Mother and Daughter)

This style has a very strong healing power for those who have suffered from separation as children, and who have lost the ability to communicate freely with their parents. In this style, the twin trunks stand by each other gracefully and peacefully, in harmony. It could be a pair of formal models, slanted models, or even literatis. Working with this style can create new avenues of exchange and a rebonding between father and son, for example, or mother and daughter.

The twin-trunk style represents unity.

Growing from a single root, this trunk then split into two trunks.

Growing from a single root, this trunk then split into two trunks.

Chinese Elm • *Ulmus Parvifolia* • Twin-Trunk Style
Mother and Daughter • 25 years old • 28" x 29"

Chinese Elm • *Ulmus Parvifolia* • Twin-Trunk Style • God and Son • 10 years old • 31" x 39"

Exposed Root

My favorite style, this specimen suggests
a tree naturally occurring on cliffs and riverbanks,
where landslides or floods have carried away the soil.
The tree's roots rise into the air five to ten inches
from the soil, and over time they acquire the same
appearance as the trunk. The trunk could be in any of
the previously mentioned styles.

This beautiful type of bonsai represents wisdom.

Exposed root, literati style

Exposed root, formal-model style

Golden Gate Banyan • *Ficus Nerifolia Regularis* • Exposed-Root Style
81 years old • 32" x 30"

Desert Rose • *Adenium Obesum* • Exposed-Root Style • 20 years old • 32" x 30"

Fukien Tea • *Boraginaceae Carmona Microphylla* • Exposed-Root-Umbrella Style • 50 years old • 28" x 29"

Round Leaf Banyan • *Ficus Mircocarpa* • Exposed-Root Style • 38 years old • 26" x 25"

Rock Cling

This style evolved from *bonsaki* (bonsai and stone in a pot), popular in the eighteenth and nineteenth centuries. A rock cling is designed in a similar way as the exposed root, but requires a rock foundation for the roots to wrap around and under. It is difficult, however, to find a tree with long enough roots for this purpose.

A rock-cling bonsai in a shallow pot is a perfect symbol of ying and yang. According to the *Book of Change*, this symbol depicts how the universe became eternal. Therefore, the rock cling represents eternal harmony.

Taiwan Banyan • *Ficus Retusa* • Rock-Cling Style
95 years old • 64" x 54"

Banyan • *Ficus Retusa* • Rock-Cling Style • 35 years old • 31" x 29"

Point Banyan • *Ficus Microcarpa* • Rock-Cling Style • 28 years old • 32″ x 30″

Banyan • *Ficus Microcarpa* • Rock-Cling Style • 28 years old • 34" x 30"

How to Create a Rock-Cling Bonsai

Supplies Needed

• Roll of wire (see chapter 7, Wiring, for appropriate size), cut into 3- to 4-inch lengths (enough lengths to attach tree roots to rock)

• Quick-drying epoxy glue or sinkers (the kind used for fishing) small enough to fit into rock crevices

• Sphagnum moss

• Muck (1/3 part clay, or heavy gummy soil, and 2/3 part shredded sphagnum moss, kneaded well—not too soft, not too crumbly, but still wet; wrap in a piece of wet newspaper while preparing the other materials)

• Ball of twine

• Container large enough to bury the rock up to the point where the tree is attached

• Basic soil mixture with coarse sand, if needed, for drainage (add 1/2 cup sand at a time until soil drains quickly)

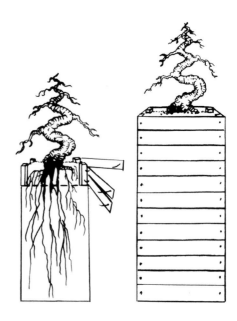

1. First, select a suitable rock. The ideal is irregular in shape, rough in surface, dark in color, and portable in size, making it easy to handle. Avoid round or square shapes, sharp breakage on the surface, and white or gray coloring.

2. Study the rock you've selected. See if it is stable on a table. Choose a front and where you want the tree to be planted.

3. Study the tree you've selected. If the roots are not long enough to form a good foundation, one solution is to build a tall, deep container with wooden slats nailed to each side. Fill it with sandy soil and plant your tree. Let it grow for a year or so, then about every two months remove a row of slats from the top of the container. As each slat is removed, the roots will be exposed, encouraging them to grow deeper and longer.

4. Remove all the soil from the roots and decide where the roots will be fastened to the rock. Cut into the root-ball partway to divide the roots into four separate directions—right, left, front, and back.

5. Bend each wire in half. Attach the bent part of the wires with epoxy glue to the rock where the roots are to be placed. If sinkers are used, drill holes in the rock instead. Attach the bent part of the wire to each sinker and place both in the hole; hammer it in to secure.

6. Place the tree on the rock and, with the free ends of the wires, wire all roots in place (during this process, keep roots damp with a sprayer).

7. Cover all roots with about one-half inch of muck.

8. Wrap the whole rock and roots with unshredded sphagnum moss and tie securely with twine.

9. Bury the whole thing in a deep container filled with basic soil-sand mixture. Be sure the container is deep enough to cover the whole rock and the base of the tree.

10. After six months, remove the sphagnum moss and wash off the muck, exposing the root formation, which is now clinging to the rock. (If the root formation is not ready, repeat the whole process and check again after another six months.)

11. Check that there has been no damage to the roots by the wires. (If there is damage, carefully remove the wire—a small groove will heal and add character; for deeper damage, use a wood dressing or sealant.)

12. Select a shallow pot or tray for transplanting.

13. Do not train for three to four months.

Raft and Root Link

These are two more beautiful styles not seen in Japan before 1955. In nature, the raft describes a tree that has fallen to the ground and, over time, has become buried in the soil, forcing the branches to grow upward like individual trees. The root link is similar to the raft, except the source of the upward-growing branches is not a fallen tree, but a long, traveling surface root that has grown sprouts. With the raft, the trunk appears much bigger than the shoots; with the root link, the trunk is more proportionate to the shoots and branches.

Many mistake these styles with the forest planting. However, a forest or group planting is several individual trees planted together. A raft or root link is a single tree that has been trained into individual trees.

The cultivation of a raft or root link is not easy, and each tree or trunk is limited by its set position. In this respect, a group planting can be easier because you can choose each tree's individual placement.

Material for these styles is limited, because some species take a long time to sprout.

Ficus and elm, however, are easy-to-sprout choices. Pine family trees should be avoided.

The raft and root-link styles represent strength and serenity.

Chinese Elm • *Ulmus Parvifolia* • Raft-fan Style • 52 years old • 43" x 24"

How to Create a Raft Bonsai

Supplies Needed

- Roll of wire (see chapter 7, Wiring, for appropriate size)
- Wooden box long and deep enough to bury the trunk at least 2 to 4 inches in the soil
- Basic soil mixture with coarse sand, if needed, for drainage (add 1/2 cup sand at a time until soil drains quickly)

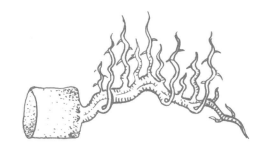

An attractive fan shape

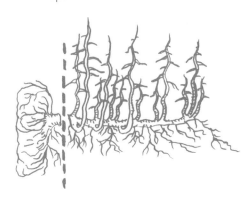

This is called "three distance" view: close-up, central, and distant. The longest branches at the original base provide a close-up view; the middle and medium-length branches, a central view; and the shortest tip branches, a distant view.

1. Select a tree and trim off any branches or shoots less than two inches long. Do not cut the roots.

2. The bottom of your tree will be the side of the trunk with the least branches. Along the top of the trunk, tie the wire lengthwise and anchor the trunk to the bottom of the wooden box.

3. Fill the box with basic soil-sand mixture so that the trunk is two to four inches from the soil's surface. (Do not bury it too deep or it will start roots on the branches, not on the main trunk.)

4. Keep the box in a sunny area. Water and tend it as you would any growing bonsai. After a year or so, roots will sprout from the trunk's bottom where the branches were removed.

5. Carefully dismantle the box to see if the roots are full and strong. Cut off the original root-ball at the base of the trunk.

6. Plant the sprouted trunk in a shallow pot so it is partially exposed. (You can plant it in a deep pot if it needs more roots.)

7. Do not train for three to four months.

Chinese Elm • *Ulmus Parvifolia* • Root-Link Style • 20 years old • 26" x 29"

Willow and Weeping

The willow design is the most poetic and romantic of all bonsai styles. Referred to often in love stories and poetry, the tree readily evokes the image of the graceful feminine form. Her long hair can be imagined to be waving gently as a breeze moves the tree's slender, hanging branches. The romantic may also envision her hair concealing a beautiful face and a tear.

This bonsai style is easiest to create with a willow species tree, as the slender branches that arise from the crown naturally fall away, growing downward and becoming lengthy. Yet almost any tree can assume this shape given a few years. While the willow grows widely along lakeshores and riverbanks in China, cherry and elm do well in both dry and tropical climates, where willow will not grow.

The weeping style displays a distinct and different ramification, or branch arrangement, from that of the willow, and the trunk can be of any major style. All branches grow upward then bend into a half circle in a downward direction, almost touching the ground. The tree species is limited; it should come from a weeping family such as willow, cherry, birch, or beech.

The pot for the willow and weeping styles should be deep with soft lines to match the soft, weeping curves of the branches.

The willow and weeping styles represent grace and romance.

Scrambled Egg • *Senna Surattensis* • Weeping Style
3 years old • 12″ x 18″

Within a few years of training, the spread of branches will begin to weep even if not a willow species.

58

Makko • *Gymnosporia Diversifolia* • Weeping Style • 28 years old • 32" x 30"

Ironwood • *Casuarinaceae Casuarina Equisetifolia* • Weeping Style • 40 years old • 26" x 36"

Russian Elm • *Zelkova Serrata Makino* • Weeping Style • 25 years old • 26" x 31"

Eccentric

Like literati, this style emerged from the Young-Zhou school, when a group of artists called the Eight Eccentrics produced landscape painting and calligraphy in a particular fashion defiant of tradition. Critics at the time regarded their work as unworthy, much as cubists and abstract painters were disregarded in the West. But observers with freer imaginations valued the art for other aspects. The artistry of the eccentrics encouraged liberation from classic art forms.

The eccentrics had their own style of bonsai—the idea was that what occurred purely "by chance" in nature constituted a singular, unique beauty. For example, if a tree developed an unusually large, knotty, or bulky trunk that dominated one's view of the tree, the eccentric would then cultivate the tree purely to emphasize this rare, misshapen feature. The eccentric might imagine, for instance, that it resembled a chubby woman holding an infant in her arms.

The Malabar tree was often preferred for this style, even though most other bonsaists of the day did not believe the tree was ideally suited for bonsai. For the eccentrics, it was their ideal. It frequently was misshapen and out of proportion. Occasionally, slender, whippy trunks of several young trees might be wound together in twos or threes. The result was topped by the combined canopy, resembling an umbrella on an unusual stem. Such forms lent easily to whimsical, interpretive imagery. To experience such imaginative freedom of interpretation was the spirit of the movement.

This bonsai style is a good model of Ch'an (Zen), or the Buddha way. It represents nature.

Umbrella Tree • *Brassaia Actinophylla* • Eccentric-Zen Style
16 years old • 23″ x 38″

Large Leaf Banyan • *Ficus Benghalensis* • Eccentric Style • 28 years old • 23" x 24"

Guiana Chestnut • *Pachira Aquatica* • Eccentric Style • Mother Holding Baby • 18 years old • 26" x 28"

Chinese Elm • *Ulmus Parvifolia* • Eccentric Style • 55 years old • 38" x 30"

Forest Planting

Forest planting is technically a group-planting style. With imagination, you can shrink one hundred miles of natural forest scenery into a portable shallow container.

This style of bonsai has become popular with international bonsai demonstrators, each using his or her own criteria. Following are the most popular methods to achieve these criteria.

Platean Forest • *Cupressus Macrocarpa* • Forest-Planting Style
5 years old • 25″ x 32″

Ling-bi Rock Bonsai Juniper • *Cupre Cupressaceae*
Forest-Planting Style • 10 years old • 43″ x 30″

Rock Mountain of Petrified Wood • Forest-Planting Style • 50 years old • 24" x 26"

Tree Materials

Most species can be used for a forest planting. Hardy trees do best with the drastic transplanting and disciplined training required. Select trees of the same species and with similar growth patterns (such as those sprouting at the same time in spring, growing at the same rate in summer, and with leaves falling at the same time in autumn). Foliage should be similar in size, shape, and color.

Size and Number of Trees

Each tree should differ in trunk diameter and height, but there is no limit to the number of trees—most demonstrators suggest odd numbers, especially prime numbers. However, my opinion is that you can use any number of trees for your forest planting as long as the result looks pleasing to the eye.

Container

The container should be shallow, such as that recommended for a rock cling, preferably rectangular or oval in shape.

Arrangement

The important elements to achieve are rhythm, perspective, and variety.

Top view

Front view

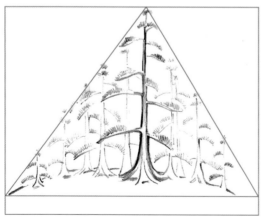

Sea-land Forest • *Cupressaceae (Cypress Family)* • Forest-Planting Style • 15 years old • 38" x 39"

Juniper • *Cupressaceae Juniperus* • Forest-Planting Style • 10 years old • 39" x 19"

There are numerous bonsai styles other than these basic thirteen. But I do not appreciate most others as they conflict with natural tree growth or shapes. For example, many people now consider a straight trunk with a particularly sharp taper as a subcategory of the formal model. The bulk of the trunk is so great for a dwarfed tree that a lifetime might be devoted to developing more ideal proportions. Also, the extreme and rigid formation seems, to me, highly unnatural.

Another example is the broom design, which, in spite of some popularity, I find quite unnatural because in nature, the snow-burdened branches commonly seen during winter do not spring upright. Rather they become bowed down by gravity, more like a willow or umbrella. Again, because this design attempts to develop an unnatural form, it lacks natural beauty.

Other styles are based on the silhouette of the trunk (straight, gnarled, twisted, split, carved, or hollow); the silhouette of the branches (windswept or octopus); the number of trunks or trees (triple trunk, sprout trunk—a single tree sprouted from a trunk, or multiple sprout—multiple trees sprouted from a trunk or surface root); or additional sea, land, or forest scenery (*bonsaki* or *suiseki*).

A beautiful style with deep wire marks on the trunk.

Composition

In any art piece, there are two basic elements: color and design. In bonsai, color is found in the buds, flowers and fruits, needles and leaves, and even in the bark of the tree. The addition of a pot complements the bonsai's color with its pigmentation and glaze, and adds form, as does the stand on which the pot is placed.

The design of a bonsai is three-dimensional like a sculpture, and it should conform to a particular style, as covered in chapter 2, Styles. This chapter addresses the overall elements of composition common to these styles.

A scholar's studio with ceramics and bonsai

Guiding Rules

Bonsai is a very disciplined craft, and the following rules are adhered to somewhat rigidly. Many bonsaists doggedly work within the confines of these rules and closely observe the conservative bonsai masters. They are reluctant to experiment with new trees and new styles. However, I believe rules are only guidelines and may be bent or even broken to incorporate your own ideas into the bonsai practice.

Roots

The root system of a tree must be developed first. Like a high-rise building, a good bonsai requires a secure, solid foundation. There should be at least five roots exposed above the soil of the pot, radiating in different directions, to evoke a sense of stability and age. However, if a root extends too far above the pot, it is thought to be grotesque and should be removed.

Trunk

The most important element of the bonsai structure, the trunk, tells more about natural environmental stresses the tree has survived than any other part. The lower one-third of the tree will be the viewer's point of focus and must have character, like that of a wizened scholar's forehead—lumps, scars, wrinkles, and twists that convey the weathering and age of an old survivor. There should be no branches on this part of the trunk. Overall, the trunk must be tapered from base to apex, and it must have a primary curve and be angled according to the style of the tree (this applies to all styles except formal upright).

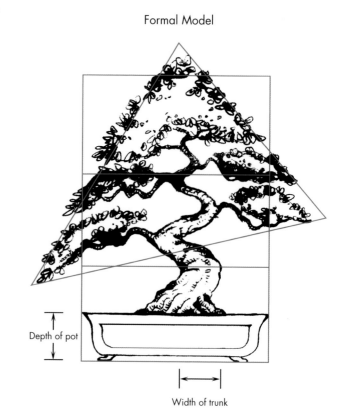

Formal Model

Depth of pot

Width of trunk

Branches

Branches must arise only from the outside of a trunk's curve—from the convex, not concave, part of the curve. They should also curve or serpentine from base to tip. No branches should point toward the viewer from the front of the tree.

The first, or lowest, branch is very important and should be smaller in diameter than the trunk's diameter. The next branch should be smaller than the first one, with each successive branch growing smaller toward the apex.

The total shape of the tree should be a triangle (whether symmetrical or asymmetrical), which to most Asian philosophers symbolizes heaven, earth, and human, and is prevalent throughout Oriental arts, from paintings to flower arrangements. Open spaces are also required for the health of the tree, as they allow in air and sunlight, and lend a very characteristic appearance.

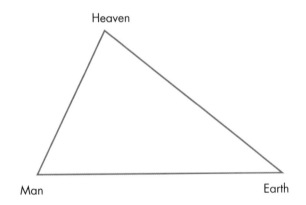

From top of tree

Top third—small branches and apex

Middle third—branch structure with open spaces in order to see the trunk

Lower third—good surface roots, open trunk with no branches

The proportion of a bonsai's trunk to its branches

The Bonsai Pot

The pot is an integral part of the final bonsai composition, and its selection is an art in itself. It must be the right size and have a shape and finish that emphasize the beauty of the tree. While there are several rules for choosing a pot, the final test is what pleases the artist's aesthetic eye.

Choice of Pot by Tree Style

Many people consider a square shape uninteresting, but dividing or adding to that square to form a rectangle produces a more pleasing aesthetic. Note that the proportion of pot to tree varies somewhat depending on the chosen bonsai style. Following are some guidelines.

pot 12″

stand 16″

Height of tree

1-1/2 of the height of the tree.

The Rule of Thirds

This is an easy guideline for selection of a pot and, in the case of the formal model, positioning of your tree within the pot. The rule of thirds is based on a numerical sequence known as the Fibonacci sequence (or "golden ratio" or "divine proportion"), in which each number is the sum of the two preceding numbers: $1 + 1 = 2$, $1 + 2 = 3$, $2 + 3 = 5$, etc. This

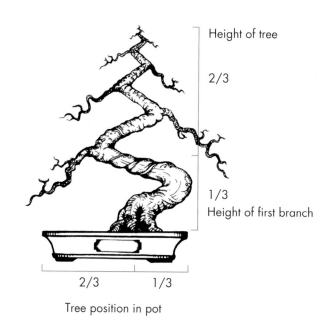

Height of tree

2/3

1/3
Height of first branch

2/3   1/3

Tree position in pot

pattern can be found repeatedly in nature—it is the increasing size of a nautilus shell that spirals away from its center, and the opposing spirals of seeds in a sunflower. For ease in working with these proportions in bonsai, it is simplified to the rule of thirds, which is only the first four numbers of the sequence.

The rule of thirds applies to most bonsai styles with the following exceptions.

Semi-Cascade and Full Cascade

Place in a pot deep enough to prevent the tree from tipping over. Also, place the pot on a tall stand, so the tip of the cascade does not touch the table.

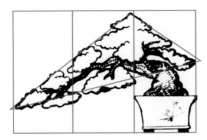

Semi-Cascade

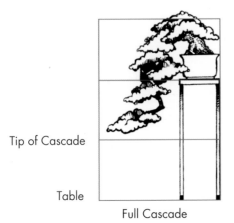

Tip of Cascade

Table

Full Cascade

Literati

Here you are at liberty to experiment, but the slender and longer trunk of the literati generally requires a deep pot to firmly anchor it. The pot depth should be one-sixth the height of the bonsai tree. Many pots for the literati style also flare out.

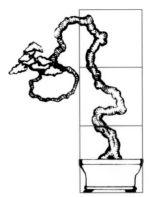

Exposed Root

Measure the trunk's diameter where the roots meld into it, which will be its narrowest part before the branching occurs. The pot depth should equal this diameter measurement.

Narrowest part of trunk

Exposed-Root Style

Rock Cling

Place in a very shallow pot, which signifies the horizon line and emphasizes the height of the rock, lending to its illusion as a mountain. While most bonsai pots should have holes for good drainage, the very shallow rock-cling bonsai pot does not require drain holes. The length of the pot should equal the height of the bonsai plus one-third. If a complementary plant is added, the pot should be longer still to give an uncrowded feel to the composition.

Rock-Cling Bonsai

Forest Planting

Place in a long and shallow pot, only as deep as the diameter of the tree with the thickest trunk. Mound the soil into a hill at the base of the "forest" to allow for secure rootage. The shallow pot emphasizes the horizontal array of a natural coppice of trees in a forest.

Forest Arrangement

Choice of Pot by Tree Type

The following chart matches tree types to pot types that have been tried and proven by the masters. If you have a tree with a large trunk that looks bulky and powerful, for example, or has large leaves, use a deep and sturdy pot. (Sometimes a landscape painting in front of the bonsai will break up the monotony of a pot this size, adding beauty to the overall appearance.) Exceptions to this chart can be made based on individual taste and pot availability.

Tree Type	Pot Type
Dainty tree with small trunk	Light, thin, shallow
Powerful tree with large trunk	Heavy, sturdy, deep
Straight, upright tree with smooth trunk	Simple, straight lines, shallow
Rough, gnarled trunk	Heavy, voluminous, deep
Sparse-looking tree	Simple, various shapes, shallow
Very dense tree	Heavy, voluminous
Young tree	Pastels or bright (but not gaudy) colors
Old tree	Traditional subdued colors, sturdy
Low-growing tree	Straight edged, inner lipped
Tall tree	Square or round, deep
Tree with small leaves	Simple, soft lines
Tree with large leaves	Heavy, sturdy, deep
Conifers	Nonglazed
Nonconifers	Glazed in contrasting colors

Pot Finish

The pot's finish should match the species of the tree and not detract from its beauty. In addition to a tree's shape and style, its flowers, fruit, berries, or foliage may also be emphasized. This can be done through color contrast or harmony. Note the primary and secondary colors of this spectral color ring.

For contrast, choose colors opposite each other on the ring. Red flowers, for example, point to a pot with a green finish. For orange berries, the pot would be blue.

However, if contrast seems too distracting, the harmony of two colors next to each other may be preferred. Similarly, the subtle hue of unglazed pottery (such as Yee-xing earthenware, from the famous capital city of unglazed pots) is also very popular. Not only does it harmonize with most trees, it evokes a sense of being close to the earth.

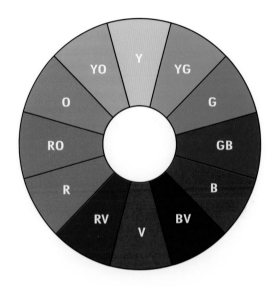

Pot Stand

The final touch is the choice of *tai*, or wooden stand, on which the potted bonsai is displayed. The stand enhances the appreciation of the bonsai much like framing does a painting, drawing a viewer's attention and focus.

The height of the stand can be determined by one of two methods: if the tree's height is shorter than or equal to the pot's length, use the first method; if the tree's height is greater than the pot's length, use the second method.

1. Measure the pot's length and add one-third to that to get the stand width (width of stand equals 1 1/3 length of pot). For example, if the pot's length is twelve inches, one-third of that is four inches; four plus twelve is sixteen—sixteen inches should be the width of the stand.

2. Measure the bonsai's height and add one-half to that to get the stand length (width of stand equals 1 1/2 height of bonsai). For example, if the bonsai's height is eight inches, one-half of that is four inches; four plus eight is twelve—twelve inches should be the width of the stand.

Most bonsai stands are made of good hardwood and are well crafted by masters. The top of the stand is usually a framed panel, within which your bonsai should be placed.

As for color and finish, it is better not to choose a stand that is close to the color of the pot, but rather one that has some contrast. However, the combined effect must be harmonious. Generally, a stand should be dark and rich in tone when polished, but not garish or overpowering in design.

Many stands in my collection are made of *tzu-tan* wood, which has a satin luster, a jade-smooth texture, and a purple-black color. This wood is valued as imperial material for palace furniture, as it is the best furniture wood. Other good woods include *huang-hua li*, chicken-wing wood, boxwood, ebony wood, blackwood, and the newest choice for bonsai stands, rosewood. Rosewood would be my last choice, however, as it does not provide the luster of other woods.

The construction and style of bonsai stands are very much like classic Chinese furniture. The style popular during the Ming dynasty generally emphasizes lines and design; it is elegantly simple and graceful. The Ching dynasty style is busier and more elaborate, with lots of carvings and inlays; it is my second choice for bonsai. A stand that is too ornate risks distraction from the tree, which should be the main focus. Remembering that simplicity is the secret of beauty, pot and stand must harmonize with and complement the bonsai.

For a tree planted in a shallow oval or rectangular pot, such as a rock-cling bonsai or forest planting, choose a low oval or rectangular stand. For a cascade-style bonsai, the stand is usually round or square, with long legs to prevent the tip of the cascade from touching the table or floor. For the literati style or *suiseki*, or if the bonsai is enormously large, a bamboo mat or slat of wood is often chosen.

When on display, each bonsai should have its own individual stand. If there is a main tree with accent pieces—a work of art, a rock, or a flower— place the accents on smaller stands with very low legs, on flat stands, or even on a simple mat.

For special occasions, bonsai may be used as interior decoration, but only for a couple weeks at a time. The following images are of living spaces of the Chinese home, displaying bonsai among other classic features.

Design

The author's main room in the style of the Ming dynasty period

The author's Ching dynasty room

The entranceway to the scholar's studio with Ming dynasty furniture and bonsai

The imperial room with a royal settee and bonsai

Age and Size

To most people, the age and size of a bonsai are of secondary importance. Like with a mature woman, it is not mere age or height but beauty, grace, and style that catch one's eye or heart. In bonsai, these alluring characteristics may or may not come with age. The trunk, for example, may achieve impressive bulk, girth, gnarls, or bark characteristics that add to its beauty and aesthetic value because these are the effects of nature. In this way, it represents a triumph of survival.

Yet there is an intrinsic worth ascribed to a bonsai of old age, which is often several times the human life span, for it bespeaks an exceptionally long and unbroken chain of more than one caretaker's devotion. Such a bonsai imposes both an honor and a weighty responsibility on the caretaker to continue this chain of devotion—or risk losing immeasurable personal honor.

To attribute special value to antiquity in the arts is also consistent with the veneration of age in both Chinese and Japanese cultures. In this regard, the old, living bonsai tree is a revered symbol. While age and size should not be your primary concerns, if you were to present your bonsai at an exhibition or convention, these factors must be taken into account.

Bonsai Size Classifications

Following is how bonsai people classify the size of bonsai.

Chinese Name	Japanese Name	Meaning in English	Size	Portability	Where Displayed
Shio-shin	Mame	Small	5–9 inches	Can carry in one hand	On a shelf, as a curio
Chun-shin	Kotade	Medium	10–22 inches	Carry with two hands	In a studio, on a desktop
Chun-da	Chu momo	Medium-large	22–35 inches	Carry carefully two men	On a countertop or coffee table
Tin-yuan shin (da-shin)	Daioromovo	Large	36 inches and above	Carry with the help of three or four people	In a courtyard

There is no limit to the height of a bonsai. In the famous Imperial Garden collection in Tokyo, there are bonsai trees more than seventy-four inches tall. I myself have a bonsai of over sixty-eight inches, and many visitors to my Hawai'i Bonsai Cultural Center have considered it the most beautiful bonsai in our collection.

Most bonsai should be measured from the bottom of the pot to the top of the apex, as the composition includes the tree, the soil, and the pot. An exception is cascade-style bonsai, which should be measured from the tip of the tail, or lowest point, to the top of the crown.

Sizes of Bonsai

1. Tin-yuan shin: Banyan• *Ficus Retusa* • Formal-Model Style
   45 years old • 65" x 62"

2. Chun-da: Russian Elm • *Zelkova Serrata Makino*
   Formal-Model Style • 48 years old • 33" x 35"

3. Chun-shin: Chinese Elm • *Ulmus Parvifolia* • Formal-Model Style
   35 years old • 23" x 22"

4. Shio-shin: Juniper • *Cupressaceae Juniperus* Communis
   Literati Style • 10 years old • 5" x 7"

Technique

Chandelier • *Medinilla Lalique* • Umbrella Style • 30 years old • 20" x 21"

Materials and Tools

Materials

Where to Find

Garden Centers

This is the least expensive and one of the quickest ways to find a tree to train into a bonsai. Your local garden center will have a selection of varieties, and the majority of them will be well suited to your climate. Talk to the nursery staff and learn all you can about how to take care of a species you are interested in. Without too great an expenditure, you should find interesting material to put into practice the techniques you are learning.

Bonsai Nurseries

You typically will not find a bonsai masterpiece for sale in a bonsai nursery. If you do, it will be very, very expensive. Bonsai nurseries basically sell stock that has the potential for bonsai training. They are an excellent source of material, but you will undoubtedly pay more than you would at a garden center because the trees have already had some training. They are, however, also a good place to ask questions.

Bonsai Club Plant Sales

Bonsai enthusiasts often propagate more trees than they can use. They also periodically reduce their inventory of trees. Bonsai club plant sales are a good source of this potential material, and another place to chat with those who have been at this hobby for a while.

Collecting from the Wild

Training of a tree begins when it is strong and healthy, as well as large enough to be worked on. If collected from the wild, trees must have time to adapt to their new environment and become firmly established. It may be years before they can be placed in bonsai pots and trained. Plus an old tree from the wild cannot be trained to any style. It would be like trying to train an old man to become a star gymnast. Therefore, collecting from the wild has its limitations—and after all your efforts, you may end up disappointed.

How to Select

The main characteristics to look for when selecting bonsai material are health, hardiness, and lack of disease and pests. The most practical tree size to start out with is one in a one- to five-gallon container. And the tree should be attractive to you—an important factor as your imagination forms the design it will soon take. Also, consider the following.

Trunk

The tree should have a well-shaped trunk, tapering gradually toward the top, and a nice bark.

Branches

There should be plenty of branches growing in all directions from the trunk. The lower branches should be strong and healthy.

Roots

Check under the surface of the soil and feel for well-distributed main roots, which should spread in all directions.

Leaves

If deciduous, the tree should have small leaves. If a conifer, the needle size is not important at this time.

Species

The species of tree should be fast growing and do well in your area. The best results come from: boxwood, buttonwood, crape myrtle, cypress, elm, ficus, zelkova, Fukien tea, jaboticaba, juniper, podocarpus, pyracantha, Surinam cherry, or any tree with small leaves or short needles.

What to Avoid

• Lanky, sparsely branched trees

• Trees that are too tall. Most styles do well with a tree proportioned like a Christmas tree, or which squats lower like a wide pyramid.

• Trees with long branches and no foliage close to the trunk

• Branches that start too far up the trunk

• Trees not suited for bonsai: African tulip, coconut, monkeypod, Norfolk pine, plumeria, and ti

Podocarpus • Buttonwood • Mock Orange • Blue Pacific Juniper • Variegated Ficus

Elm • Pyracantha • Jaboticaba • Surinam Cherry • Round-Leaf Boxwood • Cypress

San Jose Juniper • Fukian Tea • Pointed-Leaf Boxwood • Ficus Benjamin • Round-Leaf Ficus • Crape Myrtle

Tools

You do not need to buy special bonsai tools as a beginner—household scissors and a pair of pliers are good enough. If your interest in bonsai continues, however, you may want to obtain tools specially manufactured for bonsai use. The most useful are the concave cutter, knob cutter, wire cutter, and long-handled trimming shears. Following are descriptions of further tools you may want to invest in.

Potting and Repotting

A/B. Sickle—for loosening a root-ball from a pot without damaging it.

C. Root hook—for the same purpose as a sickle.

D. Rake—for removing hair roots and unwanted soil from the root-ball.

E. Soil sieve—for sieving out small articles that may clog drain holes.

F. Soil scoop—for transferring potting mix to a pot.

G. Packing stick or chopstick—for packing soil or loosening roots.

H. Drain screen—for retaining soil while still offering good drainage through drain holes.

I. Trowel—for leveling soil.

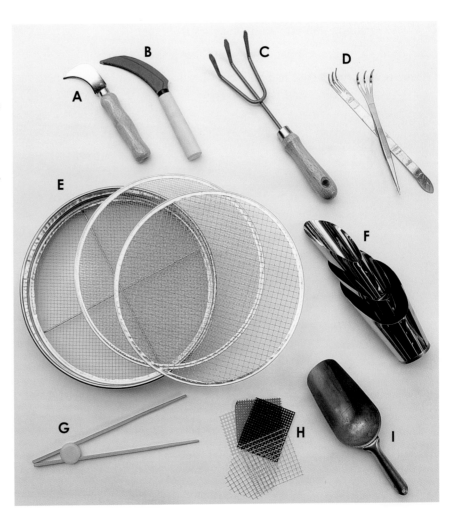

Cutting and Trimming

A. General shear to cut branches.

B. Root cutter—for trimming roots when repotting bonsai. It makes a clean cut.

C. Wire cutter—not necessarily for cutting wire but for removing wire, especially when it cuts into the bark of a trunk.

D. Concave cutter—for removing branches from the main trunk. It makes a slight concave cut that leaves no stub at the branch base and facilitates healing.

E. Long-handled trimming shears—for trimming twigs and small branches.

F. Large-branch cutter—for removing thicker and larger branches.

G. Electrician's wire cutter—for cutting wires too hard for a wire cutter.

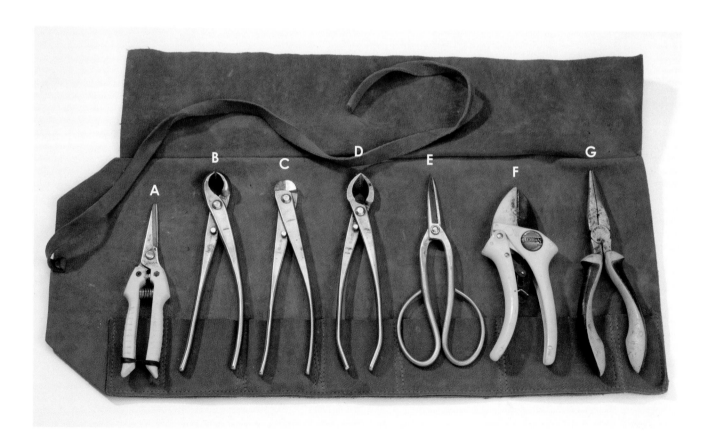

Trunk and Branch Bending

A. Bending jack—for bending a trunk or large branch too big for any wire. It works slowly by tightening a screw.

B. Easy-bending level—for bending a trunk or branch.

C. Wire—copper or aluminum (see chapter 7, Wiring).

D. Trunk splitter—for splitting trunk bark.

E. Large-root cutter.

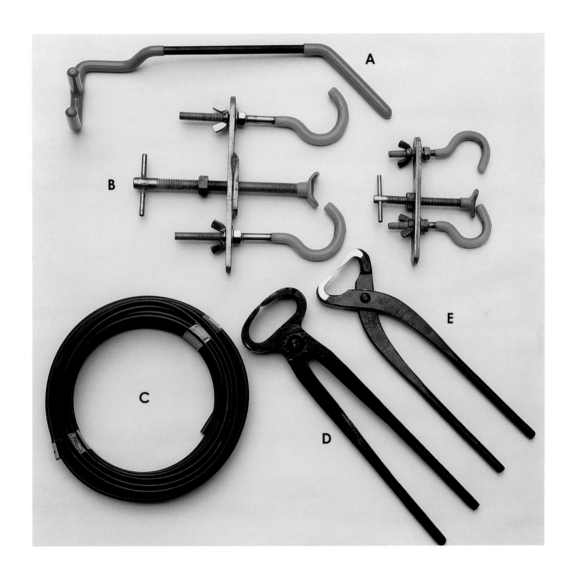

Create a Bonsai Step-by-Step

1. Select a young plant that is suitable to make the style of bonsai you are interested in making. If style is a formal model like this one, make sure the height of the plant from root to top is at least twenty-eight inches or higher, and it should

have many lower branches spread out in all directions.

2. Then wire the trunk and branches that you are going to use. Bend trunk to design and layout four branches

and the apex and eliminate the rest of the unused branches. Make sure the trunk is three dimensional and is not zig-zag, which is not recommended.

3. After three to four months when plant grows good and strong, you could transplant your bonsai to a nice bonsai pot. Fasten screen to bottom of pot. Prepare wire long enough so you can fasten your bonsai rootball to the bottom of pot.

4. Put a layer of black cinder at the bottom of the pot to provide good drainage.

5. Fasten your bonsai root-ball tight enough so that it is not mobile.

6. Apply potting soil mix and press it evenly and firmly. For a show, you can put some green moss to dress up the surface for a good look.

7. Finished formal-model style bonsai.

8. If you take care of your bonsai with good soil mix, regular watering, frequent fertilizing and lots of sunshine, in about two years, you could repot it to a larger bonsai pot and it will become a specimen of bonsai.

Training and Shaping

here are two main ways to shape a tree—pruning and wiring. (Wiring is discussed in detail in the following chapter.) Pruning is a natural occurrence in nature. Branches are constantly competing for light and air, but it is the best-placed branches that survive and grow. Branches that are faulty or crossing other limbs often die, as do weaker branches on a tree that cannot support all its foliage. Lightning, fires, avalanches, and other natural occurrences may also prune a tree or redirect its growth. Mother Nature's pruning may seem somewhat haphazard, but we can learn from her. In southern China, "cut and grow" is a shaping and training method that relies solely on pruning to achieve a bonsai style.

In bonsai, we prune for many reasons: (1) to maintain a tree's health and allow in the sunlight necessary for its growth, (2) to balance the branches and the root system, and (3) to keep a tree small and shape its trunk and branch growth.

Light and Tree Health

It is imperative that light reach all branches of a tree. In photosynthesis, light converts water and air into sugars that are then used by the tree for growth. Increasing or decreasing the amount of light affects the rate of growth. This is achieved through careful and routine pruning.

It is important to remove dead, broken, and crowded branches and twigs. Thinning overlapping leaves and small branches also allows for more sunlight to reach all parts of the tree. Remove branches with one of the cutting tools described in chapter 4, Materials and Tools.

Following are examples of faulty branches that should be removed.

Opposing Branches
Decide which branch is not needed,
based on the desired tree design, and cut it off.

Parallel Branches
When two branches grow parallel,
one over the other, cut one off.

Vertical Branches
Branches that emerge straight up or
straight down should be removed.

Wheel-Spoke Branches
When spoke-like branches radiate outward from one area, cut
unnecessary branches based on the desired tree design. (They do not
all have to be cut at the same time.)

Inside-of-Curve Branches
Branches that emerge from inside the curvature of the trunk should be cut off.

"Eye-Poking" Branches
Branches that point directly at the viewer from the front of the tree should be removed.

Crossing Branches
Branches that cut across the view of the trunk should be removed.

A tree will grow toward its major light source. Consequently, the part of the tree receiving the most light will usually have the strongest growth. If one side is weaker, face it toward the light source; auxins, or growth-regulating hormones, will be drawn to this weaker area, ultimately strengthening it.

The apex of a tree and the terminal branch buds also reach for light and will grow most rapidly. Consequently, these areas need the most pruning to keep them in proportion to the remainder of the tree. Prune any bud or branch that would make the tree's overall appearance uneven.

Root-to-Branch Ratio

The root system is basically a mirror image of the structure of the tree aboveground, so a balance should be maintained. Pruning the roots invigorates the entire tree. Combined with pruning the branches, balance can be attained.

Prune whenever you repot, when a tree is root-bound, or if the ramification, or branch arrangement, is too full or out of shape.

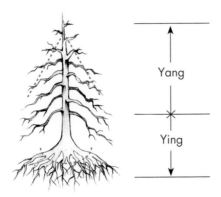

The branches represented by the dotted lines should be removed. The roots should be cut back to about two-thirds their original length. Use a root cutter.

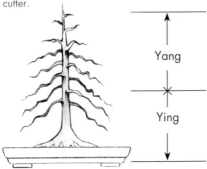

This bonsai has now been trimmed to shape. In order to balance the ying and yang of a tree, both roots and branches should be trimmed at the same time.

Trunk and Branch Growth

Pruning is a major factor in keeping a tree small, and it influences the tree's overall shape, size, and style. When pruning back foliage, remember that trunks and branches increase their diameters in direct proportion to the amount of foliage they are supporting. The more healthy foliage on a tree, the faster the trunk or branch that supports that foliage will thicken.

• To thicken a branch, avoid pruning that branch and place it toward the light.
• To maximize a branch's growth, wire its tip and carefully bend half of the wired part upward, at almost ninety degrees, to convert the terminal bud into an apical bud (a terminal branch bud located at the apex).

• To slow branch growth in primary branches, keep them cut back and turn them away from the main light source.

• Flowers, fruit, and seeds use food. Remove them to maximize branch and foliage growth.

• Foliage growth and root growth must be kept in balance with each other. If there is a need to increase foliage and girth, the tree must be placed in a larger container to accommodate the relative amount of roots.

Pruning Techniques
Thinning

Thinning is the removal of an entire branch back to a larger branch or to where the branch joins the trunk.

Heading Back

Heading back is shortening branches to the point of a bud, which will give the tree a more bushy, compact appearance.

Thinning and heading back can be done any time a tree grows out of shape, in any season. For a fast-growing tree, this could be up to three times a year.

Pinching

Pinching is the slight pruning of new growth to keep a tree in proportion; it is the primary technique for developing ramification. With pinching, the distance between leaf nodes will gradually shorten and, in time, leaf or needle size will diminish. As a bonsai begins to bud in the spring, there is a strong tendency for new growth to shoot up vertically. This should be discouraged by pinching; if not, a healthy tree will soon become tall and spindly.

Pinching is an ongoing activity throughout the active growing season. When the end of a small shoot is pinched, two new shoots usually form in its place. If, a few weeks later, these in turn are pinched each will form two more shoots. If you pinch three times in the growing season, what would have been a single straight branch is now perhaps eight little, much shorter branches.

Pinching is done by pressing soft new growth between the fingertips and pulling it free of the branch. If scissors are used instead, the tips will turn brown and many of the small buds that have not yet become active might be damaged.

Leaf Pruning (Defoliating)

This process is used to reduce leaf size on healthy deciduous trees, for all bonsai styles. After leaf pruning, the second crop of leaves will grow in a bit smaller. Defoliating also stimulates growth of interior buds that otherwise would not receive enough sun to form.

The appropriate time to defoliate is after the first crop of leaves has fully matured. In Hawai'i's warm climate, which supports such vigorous trees, the second crop of leaves may also be removed, squeezing the effects of three years into one.

To defoliate, cut off all the leaves, leaving half of each petiole, or leaf stem, in place. (It is important to remove all leaves to ensure no auxins form that might inhibit the formation of new leaves.)

Types of Cuts

Concave Cut

A concave cut is made with a concave cutter. It heals without leaving a bulging scar. Use a concave cut when removing branches from a trunk or large branch.

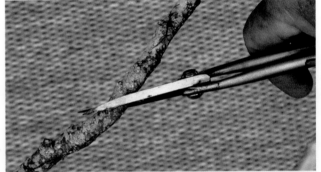

Angled Cut

An angled cut is for shortening a branch or straight trunk. It should be made with the angle facing up. Cuts made flat or facing down will not only heal slower but new shoots will emerge in the wrong direction.

1. Do not cut straight off.
2. Cut off diagonally with cut side up.
3. Do not cut with mark facing downward.

Note: On cuts with a diameter of one-quarter inch or more, apply a wood dressing or sealant. It retards rot and promotes healing, as well as discourages the entrance of insects.

Wiring

The purpose of wiring is to achieve the ideal form of a tree, enhancing its shape and style by altering the direction and position of its trunk and branches. Through your artistry, you can turn this illusion of nature into an abstract work of art that is even more sophisticated than nature.

Two types of wires are used in bonsai: copper and aluminum. Copper wire can be reused again and again, while aluminum wire can be reused only a couple of times.

Copper wire is relatively easy to use after being properly annealed (heated and cooled). It has good holding power because it becomes stiffer as it is bent and exposed to the elements. It is usually available in hardware stores and electrical supply houses. Copper wire is annealed by heating it to about 750 degrees, until it is dull red in color. An easy method is to place it on a heated barbecue grill (then turn the grill off); cover with the lid and leave it overnight. In the morning, it will be ready to use.

Aluminum wire is usually silver in color, which is not aesthetically ideal for bonsai. It is, however, also available with an anodized coating that changes its surface color to brown. Aluminum wire is easier to apply and remove than copper wire and does not need to be annealed, but it does not have as much holding power. Aluminum wire is gaining in popularity.

Wire Size

If using copper wire, the size should be one-third the diameter of the trunk or branch to be wired. If using aluminum wire, the size should be one-half the diameter of the trunk or branch.

Copper wire diameter is measured by gauge—the higher the gauge number, the smaller the diameter. Aluminum wire diameter, however, is measured in millimeters; therefore, the higher the number, the larger the diameter.

Copper	Diameter	Aluminum
#8	.128 in.	4.5 mm
#10	.102 in.	4.0 mm
#12	.081 in.	3.5 mm
#14	.054 in.	3.0 mm
#16	.051 in.	2.5 mm
#18	.040 in.	2.0 mm
#20	.032 in.	1.5 mm

The length of the wire should be 1 1/3 the length of the trunk or branch to be wired.

Pre-Wiring Care

• The best time for wiring deciduous trees is in spring, when branches are supple and soft. Conifers should be wired during the active growing season, from spring through summer. For both tree types, wiring should occur before the tree begins to flower.

• Wire only trees that are already established, not recently transplanted ones.
• Work only on trees in good health conditions, with no signs of disease or yellow foliage.
• Before wiring, do not water the tree for two days.

How to Wire

First, wire the trunk. Begin when a tree is in its early stages of growth—relatively young, slender, and flexible. Then, envision what form you'd like the tree to take in future years. Carefully assess if the trunk can be physically bent into the desired position. If it is too thick, even the largest wire may not do. Also, a thick trunk usually implies an old one, and, therefore, the danger of it splitting or breaking will be greater.

You will begin wiring at the base of the tree, near the roots, and work up toward the apex. You should always face the area you are wiring and wire toward you.

Behind the base of the tree, push one end of the wire three to four inches into the soil at a forty-five-degree angle. This will establish a strong anchor.

Use the thumb of your supporting hand to hold the wire where it emerges from the soil, and begin winding the wire evenly around the trunk with the other hand. Each coil should make a forty-five-degree angle with the line of the trunk.

Work toward the apex, moving the supporting hand to a new anchoring position after completing each spiral. Be sure the wire is not wound too tightly against the bark, or the tree will not have space to grow and scarring of the wood will occur. If the wire is too loose, however, it will not have holding strength.

• The wire should be coiled outside wherever the trunk is to be bent or straightened.

• Do not try to bend the trunk as you wire. Bending should follow wiring.

• Use heavy wire at the tree's base, medium to heavy wire at the middle section, and fine wire at the apex to avoid damaging it.

To wire branches, start on the lowest branch and work your way up toward the apex. Face the branch you wish to wire and wire toward you. Make two or three windings around the trunk; do not make 360-degree girdlings, but coil the wire at an angle. You can also secure the wire to another branch.

• For maximum holding strength, anchor the wire to the trunk above the branch rather than below it.

• To lower the direction of a branch as it grows, the wire should likewise be anchored to the trunk above the branch rather than below it.

• When raising the direction of a branch as it grows, the wire should be anchored to the trunk just below the branch to be raised.

• To bend branches down, wire over the top of the branch, across where you want the curve, and then under the branch. To bend up, wire under the branch, across the bottom of the curve, and then over the branch.

• If branches need to be twisted or rotated, wire in the direction of the twist: Branches on the right side of the tree should twist clockwise. Branches on the left side should twist counterclockwise.

• The wire should always be coiled outside the curve of the branch you are bending or straightening.

• Do not wire two branches with the same wire on the same level. They will seesaw when the wind blows, causing both branches to die.

• Wire two branches with one wire whenever possible for more secure wiring.

• Avoid wrapping leaves or needles under the wire.

General Wiring Tips

• All wires should be firmly anchored at the beginning to provide stability for the wire as bends are made.

• Wire with enough tension to provide good control.

• Use double or triple wires for more control and holding power.

• When using more than one wire, follow the path of the previous wire; do not crisscross them.

• If the bark could be easily damaged, use protective covering (floral or paper tape) on the wire, or wrap the trunk or branches with raffia first.

• Periodically inspect the wire to see if it is damaging the bark and needs to be removed.

How to Bend

Decide on the position or shape a branch or trunk is to occupy before bending it. Then place both thumbs on the inside of the direction you wish to bend; place your fingers on the opposite side. Slowly apply a small amount of pressure with the thumbs, bending gradually, repeating in several locations rather than too much in one place.

Repeat the process every few days. Remember, wires bend but branches break! Be sensitive to any increase or decrease in resistance, and listen carefully for any hint of cracking. If a trunk or branch cracks, stop bending. Decide if this part of the trunk or branch is needed for the design of the tree. If so, apply a wood dressing or sealant to the crack and wire it only enough to close the wound; let it heal before doing any further bending or shaping. If not, cut it off.

If a branch is located above the curve of the trunk, you can lower it then shape it out into a level layer.

If a branch is too far under the curve of the trunk, the reverse method should be used: raise the branch to the ideal position and then shape it.

Post-Wiring Care

Wiring a tree places it under considerable stress, so it should be given an opportunity to recuperate. Following are some tips:

• Keep in semishade for one to two weeks.
• Water heavily to restore moisture.
• Use no fertilizers, insecticides, or fungicides for one month.
• Inspect the wires periodically to determine if they need to be rewired.
• Bring the tree into full sun only after it has reacclimated.

Unwiring

Rapidly growing twigs and tender branches are usually unwired after two to three months. Trunks and more mature branches may need more time. Be sure to check the wires often. If a wire begins to cut into the bark, it should be removed. If your bonsai has not yet reached the desired shape, it may be rewired at a later date.

The process of unwiring is the reverse of how the wire was applied. (To protect yourself from the wire's springing back into your face while unwinding it, first curl the tips of any smaller wires, and bend the ends of any larger wires into loops.) Put one hand on the wire and the other hand on the branch or trunk, so the wire is under control at all times. Remove wires from the twigs and secondary branches first. Then remove wires from the primary branches. Remove wires from the trunk last.

While aluminum wire can usually be unwound, if it is larger in diameter, it may need to be cut. Carefully cut each spiral with a bonsai wire cutter without cutting into the bark.

Copper wire is more difficult to remove without damaging the tree, and is generally best cut off. If the copper wire is small in diameter and still somewhat flexible, it may be unwound.

When in doubt, it is better to cut a wire off than to risk damaging the bark.

Growth and Maintenance

Fukien Tea • *Boraginaceae Carmona Microphylla* • Above Root Informal Upright • 41 years old • 27" x 30"

Tree Identification and Care

In bonsai, we want to restrict but not prevent a tree's growth. In order to do this, we must learn how a tree grows and understand its many parts.

Tree Identification

Underground Parts

The roots are underground extensions of the trunk and branches. Their functions are:

Roots are the underground extensions of the trunk and branches.

• To hold the tree steady in the soil

• To absorb water and nutrients

• To store nutrients during dormant periods

Aerial Parts

The trunk and branches are a tree's main line of support. Their functions are:

• To provide structure—the trunk supports the branches; the branches support the foliage

• To carry water and nutrients from one part of the tree to another

• To store nutrients during the growing season

Foliage

Leaves are basically "food factories," using light as a catalyst to convert water, which is supplied by the roots, and carbon dioxide, which is absorbed from the air, into sugars. This process is called "photosynthesis." During the day, the leaves "breathe in" through small pores called "stomata"; at night they expel excess oxygen and other gaseous byproducts.

Leaves also evaporate water through their surface to allow for new water to be absorbed from the roots to the apex.

Flowers and Fruits

Almost all trees propagate themselves from seeds. Seed development takes place within the flower, which is simply a leaf specially adapted for reproductive purposes.

Layers

Heartwood

A woody layer that supports the tree, it is composed of cells less active than those found in other parts of the tree.

Sapwood (Xylem)

Through this layer, water is transported from the roots throughout the tree. Each season the sapwood is replaced by a new layer, creating the familiar "growth rings."

Cambium

The magic part of the tree that controls growth, the cambium is composed of a single cell layer just beneath the bark. In most species, it appears green when the bark is scraped. (It is orange or yellow in conifers.) The cambium layer serves many functions: it creates new wood and bark; produces new roots in cuttings, air layers, and grafts; and heals over wounds. During the growing season, the cambium layer produces a new layer of tissue on each side of it. On the inside is sapwood; on the outside is phloem.

Phloem

This layer is responsible for distributing the sugars produced in the leaves to other parts of the tree. The phloem is replaced each year, and the buildup of old phloem layers forms the thick, corky bark we see in older trees. The phloem is under the hard bark of a tree. As it ages, it becomes a new part of the bark.

Hard Bark

This outermost layer insulates the tree from extreme temperatures and protects it from injury.

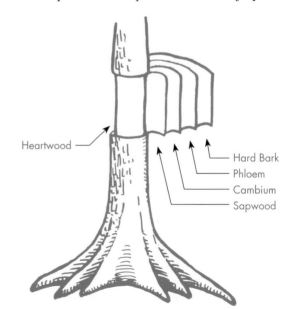

Heartwood

Hard Bark
Phloem
Cambium
Sapwood

Tree Care

The basic requirements for a bonsai's growth and health are proper soil, environment, water, and nutrients—and your attention.

Soil

Bonsai soil mixtures vary. The following standards are appropriate for most situations.

Juniper and Evergreen Trees

1 part	commercial topsoil—sifted through 1/4-in. screen; remaining grain should be larger than 1/8 in.
1 part	black cinder—sifted through 1/16-in. screen (such as window screen)
1 part	Turface (a man-made clay that does not break down easily)
1 part	peat moss—sifted through 1/16-in. screen
1 part	palm fiber
1 part	coco mulch
1/3 part	aquarium charcoal

Deciduous and Flowering or Fruit Trees

2 parts	commercial topsoil—screened as in previous table
1 part	black cinder—screened as in previous table
1 part	Turface as in previous table
2 parts	peat moss—screened as in previous table
2 parts	palm fiber
1 part	coco mulch
1/3 to 1/2 part	aquarium charcoal

Screening removes larger particles as well as fine dusts, which can clog drain holes. Palm fiber is added to increase and retain moisture and air for the root system. Coco mulch brings your soil pH to 5.5.

pH Balance

Up until recently, few bonsai books have ever mentioned a soil's pH balance—in my experience, this is more important to the life and health of your bonsai than even daily watering and periodic fertilizing.

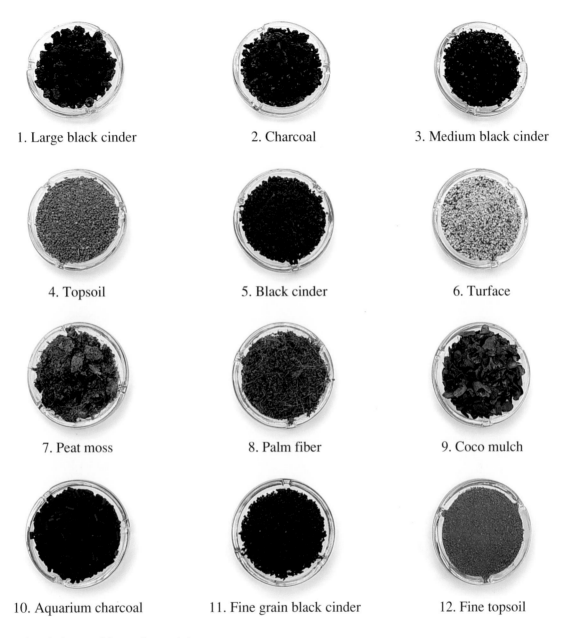

1. Large black cinder

2. Charcoal

3. Medium black cinder

4. Topsoil

5. Black cinder

6. Turface

7. Peat moss

8. Palm fiber

9. Coco mulch

10. Aquarium charcoal

11. Fine grain black cinder

12. Fine topsoil

1, 2, 3 are used on the bottom of the pot for good drainage.

4–10 are used for the middle mix sifted above the 1/16-inch screen.

11 & 12 are used for top dressing.

I believe most bonsai tree problems actually stem from an imbalanced soil pH. For example, if you see the foliage of your bonsai turn pale or yellow in spite of regular watering and fertilizing, it is a good indication that the pH is off, preventing your bonsai from absorbing nutrients. Buy a meter—check your soil's pH.

Soil pH is measured on a scale from one to fourteen—one is strongly acidic and fourteen is strongly alkalinic. The middle number, seven, is neutral. Acidity usually happens in areas with more rainfall, as it is formed by a high concentration of hydrogen ions. Alkalinity has higher concentrations of hydroxyl ions and usually occurs in areas with less rainfall.

While each species requires a different pH, this has never been defined in bonsai literature and differences of opinion abound. However, the following guidelines are accepted by most growers.

• Most species used for bonsai will grow well in neutral to slightly acidic soil (down to a pH of 5).
• The acid-loving species—azalea, camellia, gardenia, birch, and the majority of dwarf conifers—prefer a pH of 5.5 to 6.5.
• Species that prefer higher pH readings (6.5 to 7.5) include Chinese juniper, California juniper, Scots pine, white pine, apples, citrus, and cypress.

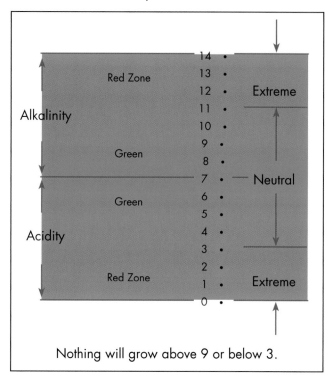

Soil pH Balance Chart

• Deciduous species have a wider tolerance of pH variations (5.5 to 8.0) than other species.

To make your soil more alkalinic, mix in more cinder or more Turface, or sprinkle lime powder on the surface and water it in. To make your soil more acidic, mix in more peat moss, or sprinkle water-soluble sulfur or vinegar on the surface and water it in. Do not change the pH level too rapidly with one application. Change it slowly by waiting a month or so to repeat the process.

Bonsai pH Ranges

Depending on the species, bonsai trees vary in their tolerance of the pH of soil. If the soil is out of the tree's optimal pH range, the bonsai may suffer and will most likely lack vigor.

'Ākia 6.0-8.0	Elaeagnus 6.0-8.0	Koa 6.0-8.5	Prunus 6.0-8.0
Apple 5.0-6.5	Elder 6.0-8.0	Kukui 6.0-8.5	Pyracantha 5.5-7.0
Arborvitae 6.0-8.0	Elm (Ulmus) 6.0-8.0	Lantana 5.5-7.0	Quince 6.0-7.5
Ash 6.0-8.0	Eucalyptus 6.0-8.0	Larch 5.5-6.5	Redbud 6.0-8.0
Atalantia 5.5-7.5	Euonymus 6.0-8.0	Lehua Haole 6.0-8.0	Rhododendron 5.0-6.0
Azalea 5.0-6.0	Euphorbia 5.5-6.5	Lemon 5.5-7.0	Rose 6.0-8.0
Banyan 5.0-6.0	Ficus 5.0-6.0	Lilac 6.0-8.0	Rosemary 5.0-6.0
Barberry 6.0-8.0	Fir 5.0-6.0	Magnolia 5.0-6.0	Sage 6.0-8.0
Beech 6.0-7.0	Firethorn 6.0-8.0	Makko 5.5-8.5	Sageretia 5.5-6.5
Birch 5.0-6.0	Forsythia 6.0-8.0	Maple (Acer) 6.0-8.0	Sago Palm 6.0-8.0
Bougainvillea 4.5-5.5	Fukien Tea 5.5-6.5	Mikimiki 6.0-8.0	Serissa 5.5-6.5
Boxwood 6.5-7.5	Fuschia 6.0-8.0	Mimosa 5.0-7.0	Spiraea 6.0-8.0
Brassaia 5.5-7.5	Gardenia 5.5-6.5	Mountain Laurel (Kalmia)	Spruce (Picea) 5.0-6.0
Buttonwood 5.5-6.5	Geranium 7.8-8.0	5.0-8.0	Sumac 6.0-8.0
Camellia 4.0-5.5	Ginkgo 6.0-8.0	Myrtle 6.5-7.5	Surinam Cherry 5.5-6.5
Candle tree 6.0-8.5	Golden Dew Drop 5.5-6.5	Natal Plum 5.5-7.5	Sweetgum 6.0-7.0
Cedar 6.0-7.0	Grape (Vitas) 6.0-8.0	Oak (Quercus) 5.0-7.0	Tamarind 6.0-8.0
Celtis 5.0-7.0	Hackberry 6.0-7.5	'Ōhia Lehua 5.5-8.5	Tulip tree 6.0-7.0
Cherry 6.0-8.0	Hawthorn 6.0-7.5	Oleander 6.0-7.5	Viburnum 6.0-8.0
Cotoneaster 6.0-8.0	Hazelnut 6.0-7.0	Orange 5.0-7.0	Willow (Salix) 6.0-8.0
Crabapple 6.0-7.5	Hickory 6.5-7.5	Oxalis 6.0-8.0	Wisteria 6.0-8.0
Crape Myrtle 5.5-6.5	Holly (Ilex) 5.0-6.0	Pine (Pinus) 5.0-6.0	Witch Hazel 6.0-7.0
Cypress, bald 5.0-6.0	Ironwood 5.5-7.5	Podocarpus 5.0-6.5	Yew (Taxus) 5.5-7.0
Deutzia 6.0-7.5	Ivy 7.8-8.0	Pomegranate 5.5-6.5	Zelkova 5.5-7.0
Dogwood 6.0-7.0	Jaboticaba 6.0-8.5	Poplar 6.0-8.0	
Douglas Fir 6.0-7.0	Juniper 5.5-7.5	Privet (Ligustrum) 6.0-8.0	

Environment

Following are tips on how to determine the best location for your bonsai:

• The best light for most trees is a full range of morning to afternoon sun (exceptions are some shade-tolerant species). Turn your bonsai occasionally, so that all sides get an equal amount of sun.

• As the number of daylight hours changes with the seasons, tree growth or dormancy is affected. You may need to change the location of your bonsai accordingly.

• Give your trees some elbow room. They need air circulation as well as light.

• Avoid placing your bonsai on the ground, where it may be subject to damage from humans or animals, as well as insect infestation.

• If you wish to display your tree indoors, keep it inside for only a day or so. Remember, bonsai are outdoor trees and need to be kept outside.

Temperature

All bonsai will stop growing if the temperature is too cold. If it's too hot, they will grow only if supplied with lots of moisture. The ideal temperature for bonsai is sixty-five to eighty-five degrees Fahrenheit. In Hawai'i, the growth rate is three times faster than in the northern United States or Canada. This means you can grow and mature a bonsai within four to five years in Hawai'i, while the same tree would take ten to fifteen years on the mainland.

Water

Water is essential for the life and health of your bonsai. However, it is just as possible to kill a tree by overwatering as it is from not watering enough.

Your bonsai pot's soil mixture should retain about 20 percent more moisture than that found in nature, where moisture and air are stored in the correct proportion for a tree's roots to function. (A hydrometer can help you determine moisture.) If the soil in a pot dries out, the tree will automatically go into dormancy. The ends of its roots will shrivel up and will stop pumping water into the tree. If moisture is not restored soon enough, the tree will die.

A tree uses a tremendous amount of water in its daily functions. A steady supply is essential to carry out photosynthesis, reduce temperature in hot weather, and transport nutrients internally. However, your pot must have adequate drainage to maintain the proper balance of moisture. Roots need oxygen as well as water; if the soil is constantly wet, the root system will weaken and eventually suffocate. The root ends will then rot and the tree will eventually die of starvation.

It's simple, when a tree is dry, give it a drink. Of course, factors like pot size, species, sun, and wind will affect moisture requirements; therefore it is a good idea to hand-water while paying attention to each individual tree.

A special can is not necessary for watering. A hose nozzle set to a fine spray is sufficient and readily available. When watering, direct the spray over the base of the tree, let it soak in, then repeat. The surface should be well saturated, and water should run out of the pot's drain holes. To remove insects or clean the leaves of dirt or soot, use a slightly harder stream of water. (In Hawai'i, there is almost no pollution, although in industrial cities like Shanghai, Tokyo, and Los Angeles, you will have more problems with airborne soot.)

The best time to water is subject to varying opinions. I prefer morning watering, which fortifies the tree throughout the heat of the day. Also, late-day watering may foster the growth of fungus, especially in Hawai'i's already moist climate.

Fertilizers

Bonsai live in relatively small containers and the availability of nourishment is obviously limited. When a tree begins to grow, it absorbs the nutritive elements it needs from the soil in the container as well as from the water and air. There are sixteen elements that sustain proper growth: carbon, hydrogen, and oxygen are absorbed from water and air; the remaining thirteen elements must be absorbed from the soil.

The percentage content of each principal micronutrient responsible for plant growth is identified on fertilizer labels. These numbers represent nitrogen, phosphorus, and potassium (often called potash), in that order. (If you have trouble recalling which number is which, remember they are in alphabetical order.)

For example, a fertilizer identified as 20-10-5 contains 20 percent soluble nitrogen by weight, 10 percent soluble phosphorus by weight, and 5 percent soluble potassium by weight. Yet these three elements total only 35 percent. The remainder consists of filler and smaller amounts of the other ten elements: boron, calcium, chlorine, copper, iron, magnesium, manganese, molybdenum, sulfur, and zinc in various chemical forms.

Nitrogen

Nitrogen strongly promotes the growth of branches and leaves. Too little nitrogen decreases growth, and leaves turn light green or yellow. Applying too much nitrogen results in overly lush growth, long internodes, and "fertilizer burn," in which leaves turn pale, then yellow, then red.

Phosphorus

Phosphorus produces flowers, fruit, and seeds, as well as aids photosynthesis and stimulates root growth. One recognizable sign of deficiency is the development of purple or red areas on the leaves, caused by the impairment of photosynthesis and the resulting loss of chlorophyll.

Potassium

Potassium ensures general plant vigor, increases resistance to disease, activates enzymes that help the plant use other elements, and counters the tendency of nitrogen to produce too much growth. The first sign of potassium deficiency is yellowing at the edges of the leaves.

Calcium, Magnesium, Sulfur

These elements also play major roles and are normally present in most soils. However, since bonsai soil mixes vary, they may need to be supplemented.

Trace Elements

The remaining elements are called trace elements, of which only a very small amount is needed for bonsai.

How to Fertilize

There are about as many ideas on which fertilizers to use, how much, and how frequently as there are bonsaists.

Organic, or natural, fertilizers have recently become popular in bonsai, but, in my opinion, trees are not too fussy about how they get their basic chemicals. Organic fertilizers include blood meal, bonemeal, fish emulsion, and ground-up seeds such as rapeseed and cottonseed. Some people are adamant about the brands they use, but I feel there isn't much difference between the major brands. The identified percentages of nitrogen, phosphorus, and potassium should be your guide.

Before deciding on the concentration of fertilizer to use, evaluate your soil's basic porosity (how fast the soil drains) and your watering practice. Some fertilize heavily, others lightly. Find out what best suits trees in your particular area. Start off by using half the strength recommended on the fertilizer label every other week, during the active growing season. If you choose to switch to a full-strength fertilizer once a week for faster growth, then it is essential to have fast-draining soil and to water more often. Use the following guidelines to aid your fertilizing practice throughout the year:

• Fertilize on a regular schedule.
• Alternate fertilizers with each feeding.
• Fertilize young trees more than old ones.
• Do not fertilize a newly repotted tree until new growth has appeared (three to four weeks).
• Do not fertilize flowering trees when they are in flower.
• Stop fertilizing in the fall.
• Do not fertilize dormant trees (during fall and winter).
• Resume fertilizing when spring growth starts.

Parasites, Pests, and Fungi

Parasites

Mycorrhiza is a parasite that lives on and within the root systems of many trees. Once thought of as a disease or parasitic infection, it is actually a symbiotic parasite—it forms a cooperative relationship with the host—and is beneficial to the tree; therefore, it should be encouraged.

Mycorrhiza attaches itself to the tree's roots and actually becomes like the tree's own root hairs. While the mycorrhiza obtains carbohydrates and vitamins from the tree, at the same time, it makes the roots more efficient and gives them increased access to soil nutrients. It does this by providing a more absorbent surface on the root system and producing acids that dissolve silicates in the soil, breaking it down into available nutrients. Mycorrhiza is also able to absorb released ions and transmit these directly to the tree. It has also been suggested that the parasite produces nitrogen and growth hormones, protects the root system against pathogens, and in the forest can move carbohydrates from one tree to another.

The importance of mycorrhiza is illustrated in an experiment where some taken from a particular tree variety was put into a blender, and the resulting solution was sprayed on small trees of the same variety. The sprayed trees showed a higher survival rate after transplanting and better growth than those that were not sprayed.

On some trees (pine, fir, cedar, spruce, beech, oak, birch, and hornbeam), the mycorrhiza is visibly attached to the outside of the roots, appearing like a fine, usually white, webby substance. On other trees (juniper and maple, for example), it is not visible, and is located mainly inside the tree's roots.

Never transport or bare root a tree that may have mycorrhiza attached to the outside of its roots. When you buy a tree from overseas, for example, the root-ball must be free of soil and media for quarantine inspection purposes. This means that any mycorrhiza will likely be removed in the process. Many trees may die after such a procedure (though this may take up to two years), since they are dependent upon the mycorrhiza for much of their nutrition and cannot reproduce more in time.

It has been suggested already that one tree can be inoculated with mycorrhiza from another tree of the same variety. To encourage growth of the parasite, however, the ideal pH range of the soil should first be adjusted, drainage should be good, and the tree should not be overwatered. Note that mycorrhiza is usually more abundant in soil with reasonably low amounts of nitrogen and phosphorus.

Pests and Fungi

Essentially, there are three irritants to bonsai trees: (1) chewing insects, which gobble foliage; (2) sucking insects, which nourish themselves on plant juices; and (3) fungi, which feed on plant tissues.

Black powder

Bubbled leaves

Deformed or chewed leaves

Chewed leaves

Chewing Insects

Name of Insect	Symptoms	Insect Characteristics	Preferred Trees and Plants	How to Control
Ant	Black powder under leaves	Cultivates aphids, scales, and mealybugs	Fukien tea and other leafy trees	Spread Amdro to kill the queen. For small infestations, spray with Simple Green.
Butterfly larva, moth larva	Deformed or rolled-up leaves	Attacks both day and night	Citrus, crape myrtle, crown flower, Fukien tea, mango, orange, and Surinam cherry	Spray with Thuricide, Dipel, or Caterpillar Control
Cockroach	Leaves or needles turning brown	Dark brown in color, nocturnal, both a chewing and sucking insect	Cypress, juniper, pine, and other evergreens	Sprinkle Diazinon crystals on the ground and spray Diazinon on the trunk
Fruit fly, melon fly	Chewed leaves, young stems, or buds	Breeds quickly	Mango, orange, Surinam cherry, and all fruit trees	Spray with Fly Killer-D, which attracts and sterilizes both sexes
Grasshopper	Missing all leaves, young stems, and buds	Flies and feeds with a ravenous appetite	All leafy plants	Spray with Diazinon, Malathion, Carbonyl (Sevin), or Isotox
Japanese beetle	Netted, deformed, or chewed leaves	Beige in color, nocturnal— The worst kind of all insects	Crape myrtle, eugenia, grape, jaboticaba, 'ōhi'a, pyracantha, rose, Surinam cherry, and yellowwood	Hard to control: spray foliage with Carbonyl (Sevin), place plant under night-light while infested, or hand-pick at night
Slug, snail	Chewed leaves, young stems, or buds	Ravenous appetite	All leafy plants, and young plants on the ground	Introduce cannibal snails, or use snail baits such as "Cory's Slug and Snail Death" (caution: harmful to other animals).

Sucking Insects

Name of Insect	Symptoms	Insect Characteristics	Preferred Trees and Plants	How to Control
Aphid, mealybug, scale, whitefly	Deformed or bubbled leaves, young stems, or buds	Secretes a honeydew fluid that attracts acid sooty molds	Boxwood, elm, Fukien tea, juniper, pine	Spray with Simple Green, volek oil, or nicotine (cigarettes soaked in water). For aphids or whiteflies, introduce ladybugs.
Earwig	Buds or roots won't grow	Eats all young roots	All plants	Spray with Diazinon
Erinose mite, mite, spider mite	Deformed or perforated leaves	Likes dry areas	All plants	Keep plants well watered. Spray with Vendex.
Leafhopper	Chewed or missing leaves, bubbled or lumped leaves	Ravenous appetite	All plants	Dust with pyrethrum, Diazinon, or rotenone
Leaf miner	Perforated leaves	Destroys plants by boring	All plants	Dust with rotenone or pyrethrum
Thrips	Deformed or rolled-up leaves	Sharp teeth	Anthurium, azalea, ficus, rose	Use systematic insect control for shrubs—after manual defoliation, mix and pour around tree roots. It will work systematically for a year.

You can also control pests through a daily application of a forceful stream of water, which will break up webs of spider mites, wash away aphids, and interrupt egg-laying activities of other pests. However, watering may also remove beneficial natural predators such as ladybugs, praying mantises, green lacewings, and beneficial spiders. Use discretion as to the actual force of spray to avoid breaking tender branches and leaves.

Fungi

Fungi can grow when the weather is very humid, when there is no air circulation, or if the drainage of a pot is poor. Signs of a fungus invasion include the trunk or branches turning moldy and black, and weakening or stunted growth of the tree.

Before treatment, try to control fungus naturally—repot your bonsai into a sandy soil mixture to maintain good and fast drainage. Place the bonsai in a high area with good ventilation and water only in the morning. If you water in the evening, the soil will stay wet through the night and support fungus cultures.

A fungus invasion cannot be controlled with conventional insecticides. It requires a specific fungicide, such as captan or Benylate. Some formulations, such as fruit tree sprays, combine all types of control—insecticides, miticides, and fungicides.

Fungi on trunk

Bugs under leaves

Other Elements

Firethorn • *Pyracantha Angustifolia* • Slanted Style • 30 years old • 27" x 30"

Jin and Shari

Bonsai is an art of illusion. It creates an illusion of age, mass, and weight to simulate the appearance of a mature tree in nature. In order to create this illusion we watch nature's forces: the dirt washes away, exposing the root; lightning strikes the trunk, making it look hollow and burnt, creating a beautiful *kunkan*. By creating the illusion of these forces through human handiwork, we can make a bonsai look one hundred years older.

In Japanese, the concept of *jin* and *shari* translates to "anchor of God." The first English book of bonsai, written by Sinobu Nozaki in 1940, describes the sacredness of this old, dead branch or part of a trunk that, when made hollow and turned gray, gives the tree a beautiful look. While Nozaki described a tree of the pine family, any hardwood tree, including junipers and hard fruitwoods, can be used for *jin* and *shari* because these woods do not easily decay due to the process.

Supplies for *Jin* and *Shari*

1. Lime-sulfur solution—for dressing and healing *jin* and *shari*.

2/3. Wood dressing or sealant—for sealing a cut (available in garden centers).

4. Wood glue—to seal surface of *shari*.

Beginner

A Dremel Multipro is good for beginners.

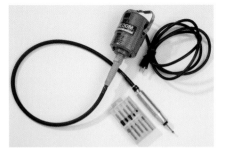

Advanced

A rotary power tool from Foredom allows for more precision.

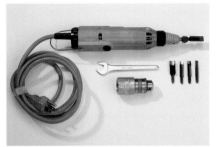

Professional

This electric wood carver is suitable for professionals.

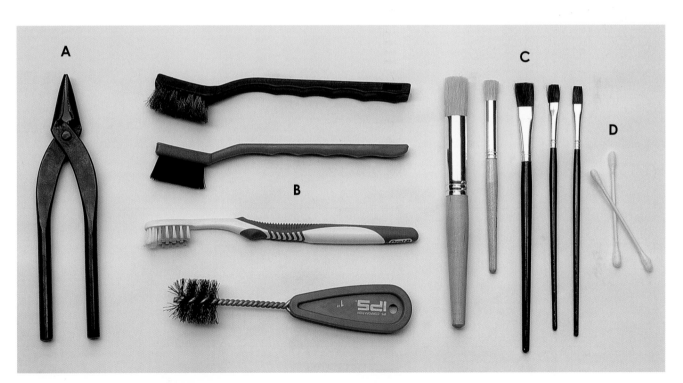

A. *Jin* pliers—for splitting bark branches.

B. Different brushes to clean and polish *jin* and *shari*.

C/D. Brushes and Q-tips—for applying lime-sulfur solution.

How to *Jin* and *Shari*

Jin and *shari* are the bonsai techniques of debarking and carving. They are used to enhance a desired composition. *Jin* is a surface carving—on a branch not necessary to the total ramification of the tree, or on a tree trunk; *shari* is the hollowing out of the trunk to form a canal.

Following are some guidelines:

• The best time for *jin* is between March and May, when the flow of sap is more active and cuts will heal more easily. However, *shari* should be done in winter when the sap flow is slow. Do not *jin* or *shari* in the hot summer, as it may harm the tree's growth.

• The sapwood of young trees and ground-planted trees is not hard enough and may decay easily after carving. Wait until a potted tree is at least three to five years old.

• Do not work on a newly transplanted tree because the mechanism of its roots may not have completely recovered yet and the tree may wither.

Before you *jin* a branch or part of a trunk, first determine where the lifeline juice flows by scratching the bark and pulling it back—if it appears green underneath, there is lifeline juice flowing there—avoid *jin* in that area, or risk devitalizing and losing the entire tree. If it appears dark or dead underneath, there is no lifeline juice there. It is also preferable to *jin* a branch with many fine branches; the tree will look more attractive as a result.

To *jin*, first carve the bark with a chisel (only *jin* one-third to one-half of the total circumference of

Select a branch that is either dead or has many fine branches to *jin*.

Use a chisel to circle the base of the trunk. Then use a trunk cutter to remove the bark. Smooth with a Dremel rotary tool and sand paper.

the trunk). Then use a trunk splitter to peel away the bark. Grind the exposed underlying hardwood with a Dremel rotary tool. Sandpaper the surface until smooth.

Apply lime-sulfur solution with a brush or Q-tip.

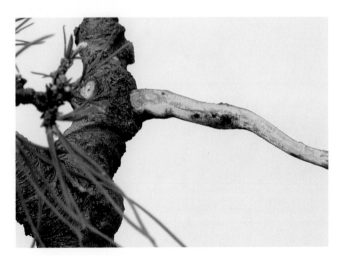

Wait a few days. It will dry and turn gray in color.

Shari applies only to the main trunk of a tree, which should be strong and vigorous. As with *jin*, you must first examine the trunk for its lifeline and avoid it. Then carve the bark with a chisel and remove it with a splitter. The trunk canal should never spiral horizontally up the trunk, but should travel straight up—a spiral is not only unnatural but will adversely affect growth.

With a chisel, hollow out the trunk's underlying hardwood into a trunk canal. If the trunk's diameter is thick enough and the wood is hard enough, you can also create a more intricate honeycombed surface with a Dremel power tool or fine wood-carving tools. Then sand the underlying surface. (After creating the trunk canal, it is necessary to watch the foliage, making sure it doesn't yellow or weaken. If

Examine the tree's lifeline and decide where to *shari*.

you see signs of fading, move the tree to a shaded area and keep it moist until the foliage turns green.)

For both *jin* and *shari*, keep the tree shaded until it begins to grow again. Wait two to four weeks for the underlying heartwood to dry (check for dryness by appearance), then apply a lime-sulfur solution. This will not only preserve the wood but, by its chemical reaction, will create the appearance of

Use a wood-carving tool to hollow out the trunk.

Apply lime-sulfur solution with a brush.

Smooth the area with a Dremel tool.

Wait until solution dries.

charring, as if the tree were struck and injured by lightning. If the solution is applied too early—before the *shari* heals over—it may enter the wound and kill the tree.

After a few days, the dried lime-sulfur solution will turn gray and look like burnt ashes.

Aftercare

Because bonsai live outdoors and are subjected to rain, wind, and sunshine, *jin* and *shari* are susceptible to decay. Following are preventative measures:

Cleaning

Jin and *shari* are not protected by bark and so are exposed to air, fungi, and pollution—all major reasons for decay. It is, therefore, necessary to clean *jin* and *shari* by washing them well with soap and water, preferably once in the spring and once in the fall.

Keeping Dry

Moisture is the primary cause of fungi. Therefore, your bonsai should be exposed to sunlight and fresh air, and the dampness of the topsoil should be carefully monitored. On a trunk with a *jin* or *shari*, decay usually starts near the surface of the soil.

Curing

Jin and *shari* should be treated with chemical compounds each time they are cleaned and dried. First, apply a quick-drying glue to increase hardness and prevent water penetration. Then treat with a lime-sulfur solution.

Rock and Stone

For many centuries, the Chinese have valued rocks and stones as objects of appreciation, especially strangely shaped ones. A closely related aesthetic form involves the gnarled trunks of bonsai trees, some suggesting a scene of nature or a legendary fairy story.

There are several types of rocks and stones that are commonly used in *suiseki*.

This mountain stone has nine divine lakes • 39" x 16"

Scholar's Spiritual Rock of Ling-bi Stone

Yin-tek Rock Mountain • 22" x 29"

Yellow wax rock • 15" x 16"

Distant mountain rock • *Sacred Mt. Kun-lun* • 31" x 17"

Shanshin Shh—Mountain-Shaped Rocks

These miniature mountains carry the power of religious or philosophical symbolism. For Ch'an (Zen) Buddhists, the rock mountain symbolizes Mount Shumi, a mythical holy mountain believed to lie at the center of the world. For Taoists, the rock symbolizes Horai, the paradise for the Taoists' spirits.

Guaishi—Strangely Formed Stones

These naturally and mysteriously sculptured rocks look like living creatures—a horse, a tortoise, a saint, a Buddha, a sea creature. Reinforcing the fascination for such objects by the Chinese is a mass of folklore about haunted stones in rugged and remote places, such as curiously shaped rocks associated with dragons, demons, and devils.

Scholars' Rocks

These rocks were worshipped and appreciated by emperors and scholars beginning in the Sung dynasty through the end of the Ching dynasty. Also known as spiritual rocks, they could be found on scholars' desks. The variety was mostly ling-bi rock, which came from Ling-bi County in the North Anhui province of China. Each rock was distinctive, with fanciful shapes evoking bizarre spirit forms.

Because of Sung dynasty Emperor Hui-Jon's love of rocks, spiritual rocks became the most highly valued objects among imperial court officials and famous intellectuals of the time. Renowned scholar and connoisseur Mi-Fei was also a true lover of rocks and is frequently depicted in his paintings bowing low to pay homage to spiritual rocks, as if he were bowing to the emperor.

Su Tong-Pua, another scholar and poet of the Sung dynasty, placed such a high value on two rocks in his collection that he would not depart from them for anything less than a pair of horse paintings by Han Kan, a famed artist of the Tang dynasty. There was then considerable controversy between Su Tong-Pua and his friend Wang Jiang-Quing about a jocular proposal by his friend to steal the rocks. The eccentric Jiang Yin Shu thought the best solution would be to burn the paintings and smash the rocks—which would be comparable to burning the *Mona Lisa* and smashing the Venus de Milo.

Mi-Fei's standard of tasteful rocks required the following elements:

• *Jion*—deeply folded and wrinkled
• *Shou*—slender and contoured, with soaring vertical lines
• *Dou*—penetrating or perforated
• *Lou*—simple and beautiful

Bonsai and Rock

A good bonsaist is always a rock lover as well. This is why when walking through a bonsai garden, you also will see many rocks—either standing alongside a bonsai pot or as *bonsaki*, in the pot with the bonsai. In a rock-cling style, the tree grows on or near a rock. In a forest planting, many pieces of rock may decorate the forest.

The same balance found in Chinese landscape painting, or *shan swei* (literally, "mountain and water" or "rock and water"), is present in bonsai. It suggests the ancient doctrine of yin and yang, where the universe operates according to two fundamental opposition elements: masculine and feminine; still rock and flowing stream; strength and moisture. Similarly, rock and bonsai represent this fundamental balance.

Another philosophy of the relationship between bonsai and rock is that both describe nature's rhythms. Bonsai keeps changing and growing. It is life and always in motion, while rock is mute, quiet, and still. As you train your bonsai, contemplate your rock—after many hours or perhaps many days, the rock may reveal something to you. The rock has stayed still, yet your human brain has been moved by this object. The feeling can bring great satisfaction to your bonsai and rock creations.

In the southern Sung dynasty, the four basic ways rocks were displayed or used in garden designs were:

1. As isolated objects, typically mounted on a stand. Special rocks were even given names, such as the Lion Rock in the Yu-yuan Garden of Shanghai, or Swirls of Cloud in the Ji-nan Garden of Shandong.
2. Assembled in groups to create a composition
3. Stacked to form a mountainscape or hillside
4. Used to create cave-like areas or grottos

Lake stones, in particular, became essential elements of the garden landscape, along with waterways and complementary architectural structures. The entire complex would take years to complete and would serve as a national treasure for centuries to come.

In 1114, Emperor Hui-Jon built a palace in the capital city of Kai-feng, with artificial lakes and fantastic formations along their shores, evoking a fairy landscape. In 1117, he commanded thousands of laborers to build auspicious hills of rocks and stones collected from all over the empire. The resulting imperial garden was considered the most luxurious in the world.

Yet historians believe that the cost of transporting the large rocks up to the palace garden eventually contributed to the end of the Sung dynasty. Because of his love of rocks, the emperor ultimately lost his kingdom.

I believe the often massive lithic lake forms found in the Chinese garden are alive. They have been said to be possessed by spirit forces from the silent depths of the waters from which they are taken. Highly revered for their sculpted and perforated forms and tactile wrinkled surfaces, they are also valued for their indefinable "ugly beauty. " The unique appearance of these stones, and their durability and permanence in contrast to the fragile bonsai horticulture, greatly complement a garden setting.

Suiseki

A rock artistry closely related to bonsai is termed *suiseki* in Japanese, literally "water stone." *Suiseki* represents a natural scene or entity, such as a distant mountain, waterfall, island, or even a mythical animal.

The art of *suiseki* is believed to have originated two thousand years ago in China. In the sixth century, emissaries from the Asian mainland brought several of these rocks to Japan. The Japanese adapted the art to their own tastes and have practiced *suiseki* to this day.

Prior to the Meiji era in Japan, *suiseki* was known by a variety of other terms—*bonseki, bonzan, kaiseki,* and *deiseki*. However, since the end of the nineteenth century, the term *suiseki* has become firmly established among Japan's large national following of the art.

Epilogue

Through my career of creating bonsai, I have preached the gospel of its spirit.

I believe bonsai's popularity and worldwide appreciation go beyond only historical and intellectual domains, and have been, in some measure, due to a universal philosophical value. It is the place within us all that appreciates refinement, which also motivates us to cultivate our highest mental, spiritual, and moral sensibilities. Bonsai pursues this cultivation, as it combines elements of art, poetry, music, religion, and literature, while being a living therapeutic art itself.

In creating your own bonsai, you will find a personal appreciation of life and nature mirrored in these unique living trees. You will find a surcease of the rush of modern life in your minutes of devotion to nurturing your bonsai. When you begin to consider how a living tree ages, how it responds to natural disasters, how it changes and regrows after trimming and training, you may reflect upon your own aging and growth, and it can have profound beneficial influences on your personal relationships.

In the past, I taught bonsai to schoolboys with learning disabilities. After only a few lessons, their schoolwork improved, they could concentrate better, they began finding value in their studies, and they were able to complete what they had begun.

In another instance, some midlife bonsai students who suffered post–Vietnam War stress disorders found the details of bonsai horticulture so absorbing that their mental disorders and depression slowly improved. The students described themselves as more mellow, thoughtful, and accepting of their world. They and their doctors believed that, in some way, their newly acquired hobby had tapped into an inner force that values peace and harmony over anger and antisocial behaviors.

Whether your approach to bonsai becomes more tangibly aesthetic or more of a pursuit of bonsai's admission to a landscape of the spirit, the practice of bonsai can improve your life. Historically, these metaphorical landscapes approach the various idealized states envisioned by Ch'an (Zen) Buddhism, Confucianism, and Taoist philosophy. And it is through meditation and creating bonsai and *suiseki* that you can reach these philosophical goals. It is an intuitive and seemingly contradictory approach: To gain a broader understanding of life, you must yield your dependence on trivialities. To grasp the greater truths of the universe, you must let go of self-imposed limitations. To attain peace and a spiritual bond with nature, you must lose the fear of change.

When you work with a pot of bonsai, you are working with the entire universe. This is the illusion of bonsai.

Glossary of Terms

Apex—The upper tip of the tree.

Auxin—A growth-regulating hormone produced at the apex and at branch tips, where cells actively divide. Auxins flow into the stem, lengthening the first internode, and move down to stimulate formation of lateral buds and the growth of roots.

Axillary Bud—A new bud, which bears a protective coating, that will replace a nearby leaf or branch at its last location.

Blade—The flat portion of the leaf.

Lateral Bud—A bud that grows between the trunk and the apex.

Node—A joint on the trunk or branch where growth begins. There are two kinds of nodes: leaf and flower. An internode is the distance between two nodes.

Petiole—The stem of the leaf blade.

Ramification—The arrangement of the branches.

Stomata—The small pores on the leaves through which leaves take in air.

Terminal Bud—A bud located at the apex (also termed an apical bud) as well as at the end of a branch.

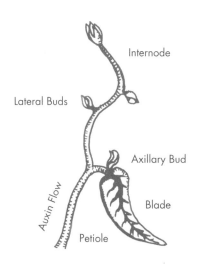

Judging Bonsai

Bonsai critiques are intended to improve the quality and standards of bonsai—individually and collectively. A critique can enhance your enthusiasm for your bonsai work, or give constructive direction to its improvement. Although there is formal judging at bonsai association gatherings and conventions, you should learn to critique your own trees. We are all students at some level and can derive pleasure from both the result and the effort of the study.

Your critique should follow the criteria of chapter 3, Composition. It should also follow the principles of bonsai appreciation shown below:

• Bonsai is inspired by nature, but is more abstract than nature.
• Though created by the human hand, bonsai should appear to be formed by nature.
• There should be clear distinction between primary and secondary branches.
• Integration and variation should be unified.

• All bonsai elements should be in the appropriate proportion.

The following pages are a rather extensive assessment form typical of a formal judging. Note how various points are examined.

Bonsai Critique

Specie of the tree:		Style:			
Owner:		Critic:		Date:	
			Poor	Good	Excellent
1. Trunk	Curvature to style				
	Taper gradually				
	Bark condition				
	Character of lower third				
2. Branches	Development				
	Size of primary branches				
	Size of secondary branches				
	Size of ternary branches				
	Integration				
	Variation				
3. Foliage (Leaves)	Health				
	Proportion				
	Ramification				
	Compaction of twigs				
4. Roots	Butt (visibility above soil)				
	Radiation				
	Five or more				
5. Apex	Triangular shape				
	Aesthetic appearance of twigs				
	Proportion				
	Balance				
6. Soil	Finish (moss or sand)				
	Other				
7. Pot	Size (proportion to tree)				
	Shape (harmony with tree)				
	Finish (harmony with tree)				
8. Stand	Style harmony	• with pot			
		• with tree			
	Shape and size				
	Finish harmony	• with pot			
		• with tree			
9. Overall aesthetic appearance:	Harmony of tree, soil, pot, and stand				
Remarks					

About the author

Through over fifty years of bonsai cultivation and research, Walter Liew has accumulated one of the largest bonsai collections in the world. (All of the bonsai pictured in this book are from the author's collection.) At his Hawai'i Bonsai Cultural Center, located on the Waimānalo countryside of Honolulu, one can also find substantial *suiseki* and garden rock collections, artworks, and rare Chinese furniture and antiques.

Born in China's Shandong province, Liew was educated in Taiwan and received firsthand training on the priceless artworks and national treasures of the Palace Museum collection from Beijing. Under the supervision of classical scholars and museum curators, Liew gained a foundation of Chinese culture and art forms which he has used throughout his life.

Today he can be found working, teaching, and relaying in colorful detail a keen personal knowledge of bonsai and history, art, and philosophy—in both Mandarin and English. He also teaches bonsai classes at the Windward Community College.

Bibliography

Covello, Vincent T. and Yuji Yoshimura. *The Japanese Art of Stone Appreciation: Suiseki and its Use with Bonsai*. Tokyo: Charles E. Tuttle, 1984.

Forrer, Matthi. *Hiroshige*. Munich, New York: Prestel-Verlag, 1997.

Forrer, Matthi. *Hokusai*. Munich, New York: Prestel-Verlag, 1991.

Han, Pao-Teh. *External Forms and Internal Visions: The Story of Chinese Landscape Designs*. Translated by Carl Shen. Taipei: Youth Cultural Enterprise, 1992.

Koreshoff, Deborah R. *Bonsai: Its Art, Science, History and Philosophy*. Portland: Timber Press, 1984.

Naka, John Yoshio. *Bonsai Techniques II*. Santa Monica: Dennis-Landman, 1984.

National Palace Museum. *Masterpieces of Chinese Figure Painting in the National Palace Museum*. Taipei: National Palace Museum, 1973.

Nippon Bonsai Association. *Classic Bonsai of Japan*. Tokyo, New York: Kodansha International, 1989.

Okimoto, Elaine. *Bonsai in Hawaii*. Illustrated by Paul Imada. Honolulu, 1990.

Ribeiro, Susan, ed. *Arts from the Scholar's Studio*. Hong Kong: The Oriental Ceramic's Society of Hong Kong, 1986.

Samson, Isabelle and Remy. *The Creative Art of Bonsai*. First English Paperback Ed. West Sussex: Ward Lock, 1991.